A DOLLAR MORE

A DOLLAR MORE

MABLE GULLEY-HARVEY
& BRAD HARVEY

*To Aunt Ruby Aaron who was present at the birth of
all seven of my mother's babies including me.*
– Mable Gulley-Harvey

*For Nikki, Kristin and Josie, may you always lead lives
worth writing about.*
– Brad Harvey

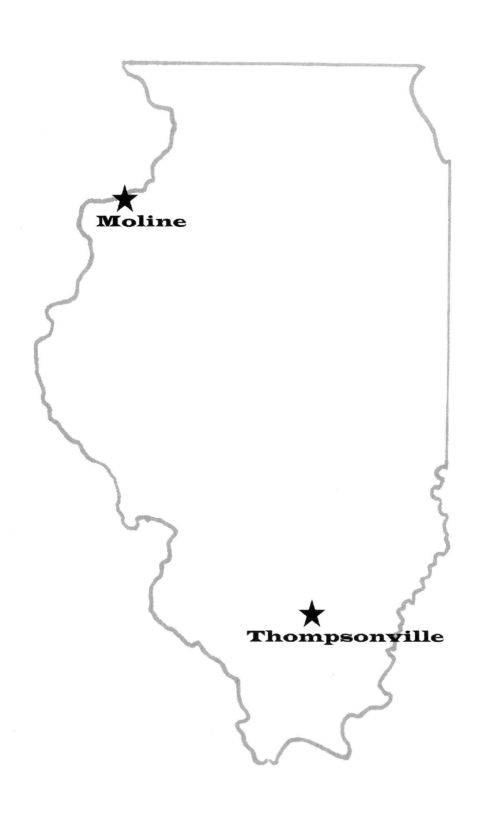

TABLE OF CONTENTS

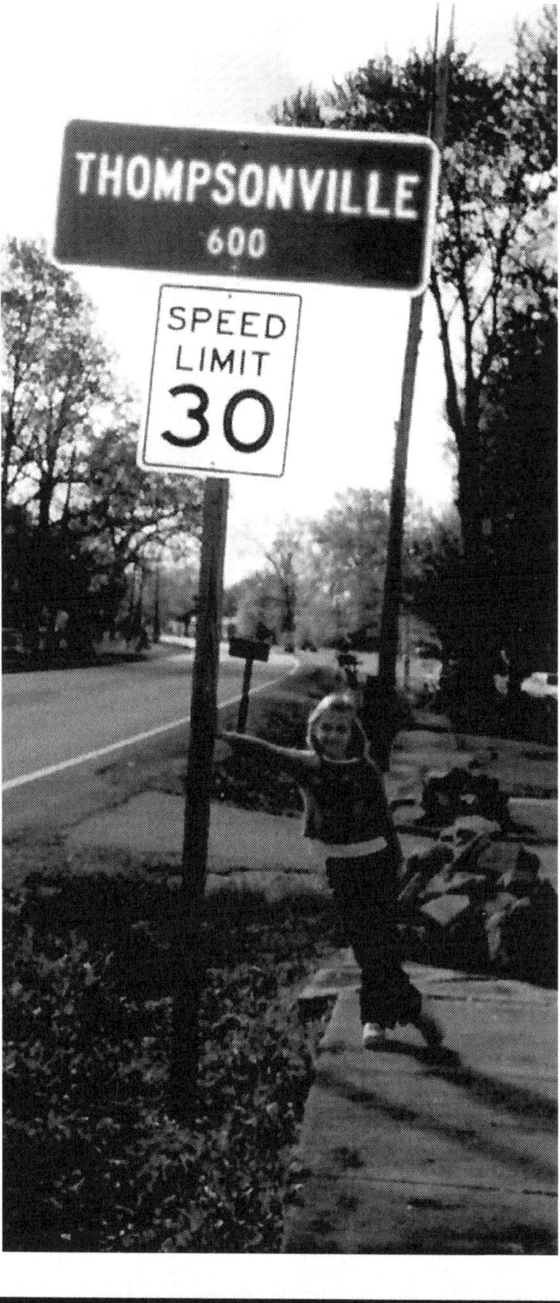
THOMPSONVILLE
600
SPEED
LIMIT
30

FOREWORD

This is YOUR story.

Yes, you...the person who is holding this book in your hands, wondering whether you'll connect with it.

Of course you will.

It's a story about an America that your grandparents or parents told you about. It's the story of two families, the Gulleys and the Harveys, and their Illinois origins.

But these are the stories you've heard, too. Because someone has told you the story of your grandparents, or your own uncle, or maybe your brother who defied odds against survival with the grit of their own will and the support of family members as tough as they were.

In this America, women toughed it out when they lost a child. "Have another baby," was the doctor's recommendation.

In this America, you could have a garage built secretly without your husband knowing a thing about it.

In this America, you could hitchhike.

In this America, you could drive through a desert in a car without air conditioning.

In this America, you toughed it out with determination, hard work and love for your family, your friends and neighbors.

They are the stories of the Harveys and the Gulleys, the families who were tough, determined and able enough to make it through some of the most challenging times this nation, and the Midwest, ever have known.

Perhaps your last name isn't Gulley or Harvey. Still, this is the story of you – of your grandparents, or their parents – and the people you know, who didn't always have enough money, didn't always have enough to eat, didn't always have the means to make their dreams come true.

But they always had the grit and the will to not only survive, but also to create an incredibly warm environment of family and friends who remained loyal to each other through the most trying of times.

It is the story of America that you hold in your hands.

-LINDA COOK
2018

The Amos Calhoun Harvey family, circa 1919. Back row: Vernor, Robert.
Middle row: Velma, Nancy (wife), Amos. Front Row: Don, Ruth.
Nancy was pregnant with their final child Roberta.

PREFACE

Brad Harvey

I was having a conversation with my cousin about the volatile relationship between her late parents when she casually remarked that there was a bullet hole in the wall of her former family home.

"Mom took a shot at dad but missed," she said nonchalantly, the passage of years having rendered the scandalous incident into a mundane anecdote. "They laughed about it later and hung a picture over the hole to remind them not to ever let their anger go that far again."

My aunt and uncle generated some of the most colorful tales in our family's history. Each had horrible tempers that respected neither bystanders nor boundaries when triggered and it was a matter of dumb luck that they didn't accidentally kill each other or any innocents that happened to stray into their war zone.

An argument between neighbors over a broken headlight escalated into an assault on my aunt and my uncle. My uncle chased the guilty party on foot through their farming community before he decked the man in the mezzanine of the local bank (another version of the story has my uncle knocking him out inside the post office). For their part in the altercation my aunt and uncle were handcuffed and taken to jail.

When my aunt once suspected my uncle of having an affair, she drove his pickup truck to the small town where the alleged tryst occurred, pulled off to the side of the highway and waited. My uncle, traveling the same route home in his four-cylinder

Omni, thought little of the parked pickup until it roared up from behind and slammed into the rear of his vehicle, commencing into a high-speed game of bumper-tag between husband and wife. While he was stopped at an intersection my aunt hit him hard, the impact from the truck sending his car into oncoming traffic.

By the time my aunt had pulled the battered Chevy into the driveway of their house my uncle already had disappeared inside. Fearing his temper,

Jessie and Robert Harvey Sr.

she stayed in the truck the remainder of the night until she was greeted at dawn by my uncle, holding a gasoline can and lit cigarette lighter, threatening to torch the truck with her in it. A few days later my aunt, an amateur artist with her work hung throughout the house, found pieces of the truck's grill methodically hammered into her paintings.

Or at least that's what I've heard. Subsequent retellings by family over the decades may have rendered specific details apocryphal, though I'm certain arrests were made and bits of Chevy got retrofitted to some otherwise-benign artwork.

In deference to my cousins, not all of whom are enamored with the baser aspects of their parents' behavior, I've left out names (I should add that my aunt and uncle morphed into a lovely couple in their later years, serving up many a bologna sandwich and homespun yarn whenever I visited).

My uncles are—and were—the best storytellers I've ever known. Seated around my parents' kitchen table with a pot of beans boiling on the stove (a Gulley staple) and cigarette smoke heavy in the air (another Gulley staple), they could entertain for hours. I've always been in awe of those who could recite

Amos and Nancy in the mail wagon with their children.

swaths of their family history at random. But as my mother and I labored over the writing of this book, we learned that auto accidents have many eyewitnesses and dead men tell no tales. And apocryphal is as apocryphal does.

* * * * * * * * *

When I was a child, the 350-mile journey from our hometown in Moline, Illinois to my parents' hardscrabble beginnings in rural Thompsonville, Illinois was winding and arduous by car before the modern-day interstate system allowed my parents to shave off a few hours of travel time. The trek began in Milan on Route 67 and wound south through Monmouth, Macomb, Rushville and Beardstown. A few turns later we were cruising southeast through Springfield, Taylorville, and Pana before veering south through Vandalia, Centralia and Mt. Vernon.

It would be dark and I was usually asleep in the back seat when my parents would pull into West City, a suburb of Benton, Illinois where my great aunt, Ruby Aaron, resided. After the obligatory courtesy visit, we would drive the final 10 miles to Thompsonville to the home of my paternal grandparents, where I would slip between the musty sheets of a lumpy sofa bed in the living room and finish my broken sleep. I would awaken to the sound of adults conversing and the radio broadcasting farm reports, the house smelling of brewed coffee and burnt bacon. Still in my underwear I would dart into the bathroom to shower with ancient bars of rust-streaked green soap and dry off with threadbare towels. I was thankful for indoor plumbing because my grandparents' previous address had an outdoor toilet (e.g. outhouse) that was miserably cold during the winters and insect-infested through the summer heatwaves.

My grandfather Robert Harvey Sr. had been up and gone for hours to tend to his feed store—the man never slept past 4 a.m. and loved his long solitary pre-dawn walks — while my grandmother Jessie for a time pulled shifts behind the counter at the local post office (she would be forced into retirement at age 75). My parents would have a full day catching up with old friends and relatives, leaving me to amuse myself however I saw fit. I always brought plenty of comic books and art supplies. Later I would refurbish a bicycle found in my grandparents' shed and explore the county back roads. I never made any friends in Thompsonville. Rather like the bemused Oliver Douglas on the television sitcom "Green Acres," I was too different to mesh comfortably with the locals.

* * * * * * * * *

While the Gulleys were essentially renters and laborers, the Harveys owned property, were well-educated and beacons of the community. My great-great-great-grandparents Elijah Bell and Catherine Harriet (Bare) Harvey were farmers in Woodlawn, Illinois, a village in Jefferson County near Mt. Vernon. Catherine Harriet

Harvey would donate the land on which Mt. Catherine Christian Church would be built in Woodlawn, along with the adjoining property that would become the Mt. Catherine Cemetery, both named for its benefactor. Elijah and Catherine's son, my great-great-grandfather Pleasant L. Harvey, would marry Mary Katerine Moore ("Katerine" possibly Americanized later to "Catherine") and the union would produce 13 children, including the eldest, my great-grandfather Amos Calhoun Harvey.

Amos was clearly ambitious, working the farms of his parents and grandparents while serving two terms as clerk of Casner Township (established in 1861, the township organization boasted several Harveys on its board, including Amos' grandfather Elijah). While employed as a door-to-door salesman he met Nancy Elizabeth Gardner and the two wed on July 17, 1898, the same year he received his teaching certificate. Amos actively taught throughout the area, finding time to open a general store in nearby Sesser in 1907 (it would close within a year). He followed his teaching profession to Thompsonville in 1914.

With a growing family to support, Amos opted for the security of a full-time position with the United States Postal Service, becoming a rural mail carrier in 1915. He never quite mastered the complexities of the Model A automobile, preferring to employ a series of drivers (usually relatives or townspeople hired on the spot) to chauffeur him on his daily mail rounds except on inclement days when muddy, rutted roads required delivery by horse and buggy. He kept the job for 25 years until his retirement in 1940, finding time to open the Harvey Tire Company of Thompsonville, where he would exhibit an encyclopedic knowledge of various tire brands and their respective tread depths for his customers. During his sunset years he would remain a fixture at school athletic events and was a particular fan of professional wrestling, attending bouts in Evansville, Indiana with my 16-year-old father along as companion and driver. Arthritis and other maladies would confine Amos to bed during the final three years of his life until he passed away on April 3, 1951 at the age of 75.

* * * * * * * *

On July 22, 1977, I was performing a weekend gig with my band in Matherville, Illinois when my parents received word that Robert Harvey Sr. had died from a heart attack. While my band mates packed up the gear, my parents duly picked me up on their way out of town for the all-night drive to Thompsonville.

It had been only a few years since we'd buried my great uncle Opal Flannigan, a burly giant with a booming voice whose bad knees and inverted stick legs made him look top-heavy. Opal had married Jessie's younger sister Helen after her rancorous

Left: Robert Harvey Sr. Center: Helen White, age 20. Right: Jessie White, age 20.

divorce from Ray Cook, a local railroad engineer who fathered my second cousin Jerry and whom Helen decried "had a girlfriend in every station." Opal had once served as an orderly in a mental hospital, a profession that appealed to Opal's bawdy sense of the absurd. He ran successfully for mayor of Thompsonville and was in office when the tornado hit the town in 1971, nearly killing my grandfather Harvey when the winds pulled him out along with the wall of my uncle Bill Harvey's veterinarian office. After Illinois Governor Richard B. Ogilvie arrived to assess the damage and present the town with a $20,000 disaster relief check, Opal slipped it into his wallet and held onto it for weeks. "Hey Bradley Joe," he'd say to me while patting his back pocket, "Want to see a check with a lot of zeroes on it?"

The funerals of my great-uncle and my grandfather gave me some insight into the irreverence of their widows. I was riding in the second car of Opal's funeral procession with Jessie and though I don't recall exactly what she was saying I do know it was highly inappropriate, albeit outrageously hilarious. So much so that by the time the graveside service commenced I was sufficiently primed a la the "Chuckles the Clown" episode of the "Mary Tyler Moore Show" in which Mary struggles to stifle her laughter during a solemn funeral ceremony. Opal was buried with military honors. By the time the bugler delivered the worst-sounding version of "Taps" this side of Radar O'Reilly, I was standing behind grief-stricken Helen chewing my shirt collar in order to muffle an uncontrollable fit of giggles.

Helen was no less impious during my grandfather's service. She held court in the second funeral car, elaborating on how Jessie had defied my grandfather's burial wishes and "yanked him" from his preferred resting place at Mt. Catherine's in Woodlawn and instead "planted him" in the Masonic and Odd Fellows Cemetery in Benton. She intimated Jessie had done the switch in retaliation for my grandfather's $10,000

Jill Harvey with Robert Harvey Sr.

purchase of the building that housed his feed business, bought at the time without Jessie's knowledge or consent. Despite the timbre of the times, when women were expected to accede to the wishes of their husbands without question, neither sister suffered fools gladly.

* * * * * * * * *

Robert Earl Harvey (a name he would pass down to my father) entered the world on March 3, 1899, the eldest of six children born to Amos and Nancy (followed by Vernor, Velma, Ruth, Don, and Roberta, in birth order). Unlike Amos, who combined education with entrepreneurial skills to avoid the hard graft of the area's coal mines (the region's biggest employer), Robert left school after sixth grade and entered the mines at age 12. He would stay until 1917 when he was drafted into the United States Infantry and sent overseas during World War I. While serving in France he was gassed during a skirmish in the Meuse-Argonne Forest, a battle that claimed 26,277 American lives and became one of the deadliest in American history. For his service, Robert obtained a Victory Medal.

Discharged from the military on May 31, 1919, Robert returned home to work in the mines for several years before leaving the profession altogether due to breathing problems exacerbated by the coal dust (he would claim shortness of breath before and after his stint in the mines but also thought exposure to an unknown chemical agent—the gassing during the war—further damaged his lungs).

After marriage to Jessie and the birth of their two sons he acquired a service station from his in-laws, did farm work for $1 a day and became a prison guard in Chester, Illinois. He ran Harvey's Feed Store in Thompsonville until his first major heart at-

Tallest man in Thompsonville: Opal Flannigan served as mayor during the early 1970s. Illinois Governor Richard Ogilvie (far right), in Thompsonville to survey damage from the 1971 tornado.

tack forced him into an early retirement, when he would draw a combination of Social Security benefits and a veteran's disability pension connected to his World War I service (though he would apply several times to receive black-lung benefits his claims were denied). His final years were spent running the office of his son's veterinarian practice while retaining active memberships in the American Legion of Thompsonville, the Akin Masonic Lodge No. 749 and the World War I Barracks in Benton.

My sister, born nearly a decade ahead of me, remembered my grandfather Harvey as "always full of big hugs." We both recall his nightly ritual of winding the clock above the mantel before bed. He shared his interests with the two of us although fishing was not my thing (I was horrified the first time I watched him take a pocketknife and behead a turtle hooked on a trot line).

But I give my grandfather credit for making the effort to connect with his bookish city-bred grandson. Notorious for his last-minute holiday shopping—Thompsonville on Christmas Eve would never be a cornucopia for discriminating gift-givers—he showed up with a Tot stapler so I could piece together the homemade comic books I'd been drawing, which proved to me he was paying attention after all.

The adult children of Amos and Nancy Harvey. Left to Right: Don, Velma, Ruth, Robert, Vernor, Roberta.

A teenage Josie Aaron.

1

DARLING MOTHER

Mable Gulley-Harvey

My mother Josephine (Josie) Evelyn Aaron was born Oct. 9, 1906, the youngest and only girl in a family of six children. The daughter of Henry and Emma Jane Aaron of Thompsonville, Illinois, she had a twin brother, Joseph (Joe). But sadly, two other brothers, Billy and Roy, would die in childhood.

More tragedy would follow as Henry went blind when infection set in after cataract surgery. He would eventually be one of 20 to 40 million victims of the worldwide influenza pandemic of 1918. My mother was 12 at the time.

With their mother widowed, Josie and Joe found themselves responsible for earning a portion of the household income. Their elder brothers Reg and Rex, lifelong illiterates and alcoholics, spent their school years skipping classes, drinking and fighting—my mother managed to teach Reg how to write his name so he could at least cash his payroll checks on the occasions he found work. Meanwhile, she earned as little as five cents per night as caretaker for an elderly shut-in.

* * * * * * * * *

On March 18, 1925, what became known as the Tri-State Tornado touched down in Missouri. A monster storm, it barreled through portions of the state, clocking winds estimated at times in excess of 300 mph. After leveling several communities in its path, the tornado crossed the Mississippi River into southern Illinois where it wiped out the town of Gorham before moving onto Murphysboro and De Soto.

Four-year-old twins Josie and Joe flank their mother, Emma Jane Aaron.

When it reached West Frankfort, the storm, in addition to destroying homes and businesses, blew over a multi-ton coal tipple [a type of chute used to load coal into railroad cars] while railroad tracks were ripped from the ground. The tornado obliterated the small town of Parrish, then proceeded to devastate rural areas of Hamilton and White counties before crossing the Wabash River into Indiana. There the towns of Griffin, Owensville and Princeton suffered considerable damage before the storm dissipated near Petersburg.

The tornado had remained on the ground for more than three hours. At least 695 people died, and 2,027 more were injured, the majority in southern Illinois.

Although the tornado had missed my mother's hometown of Thompsonville, she never forgot the sight of the train backing its way from Thompsonville to Parrish through all the debris covering the rails. Casualties of the storm were loaded onto flat-bed cars and transported to morgues in neighboring communities. The memory terrified her. Throughout her life during thunderstorms she would pace and search the skies for funnel clouds.

While still in her youth my mother contracted scarlet fever, necessitating a family quarantine. Neighbors would leave food and medicines on the porch. The illness robbed her of her hair so she wore a dust cap to hide her baldness when she returned to school. When her hair grew back it was curly and a beautiful shade of red.

My mother was a slender woman of 5'8" when she met Lawrence John Gulley. And I believe that after the tragic events in her life, when she met and fell in love it was a very happy time.

She was working as a maid at a small hotel in Thompsonville when Lawrence came in looking for work.

Josie and Lawrence Gulley.

After a brief courtship they were married Feb. 4, 1928, by a justice of the peace in Benton, Illinois.

* * * * * * * * *

Franklin County was notoriously violent throughout the 1920s because two rivals, the Shelton Gang and a Russian Jewish immigrant named Charlie Birger, fought for control of the area's bootleg liquor, gambling and prostitution. Birger held a particular hatred for the Ku Klux Klan, another unsavory player in the gang wars between the factions. Ultimately, Birger was implicated in two failed murder attempts against West City Mayor Joe Adams and sentenced to death by hanging April 19, 1928.

My mother was two months pregnant with me and on hand to witness the last public execu-

The Gulley boys. Back row: Joseph Charles, Bobby, Donald Eugene. Front row: Lawrence Edward, Arthur Lee, Billy Bob.

tion by the State of Illinois. The event drew an estimated crowd of 5,000 outside the Benton jail. Onlookers—many brought their families—watched Birger shake hands with the hangman before having a black bag placed over his head. Reportedly, before he was dropped through the trap door, he uttered "It's a beautiful world!" His death marked the end of a bloody and lawless era in Franklin County.

* * * * * * * * *

I believe my father wanted a large family because he had been an only child whose parents divorced when he was 4, leaving him to grow up in his grandfather's home. My mother loved the idea because she loved my father, probably never dreaming how hard it would be to raise a large family in the midst of the Great Depression.

There were six boys after me, two and three years apart, all born at home (Joseph Charles, Bobby, Donald Eugene, Lawrence Edward, Arthur Lee, and Billy Bob, in order of birth). Aunt Ruby was seven years younger than my mother and married to Joe. She remained my mother's closest friend and was there at the birth of all my brothers and me.

My mother never bothered with doctors until the birth of each baby was imminent. When she went into labor my father would stop by Aunt Ruby's and tell her, "Josie said for you to come out today." Then he would go on to work while Aunt Ruby would contact the doctor who would come to our house and deliver the baby. She

Joe and Ruby Aaron with their sons, Lavern, Billy Gene and Bobby Joe.

would take the newborn from the doctor, bathe it, and once assured of the baby's well-being, comfort my mother post-partem. My father was not always at the birth of his children but Aunt Ruby was.

We seldom saw doctors while we were growing up. Of course we had full-strength aspirin on hand and there was a big blue jar of Vicks used for colds. My mother would slather an 18 inch square of flannel with the stuff, slap it on my chest and back and leave the square under my pajama top overnight until the cold symptoms vanished. For earaches my father would light up his pipe and blow warm smoke into my ear to break up any waxy residue. He treated sore throats by placing a drop of turpentine on a teaspoon of sugar and making us swallow. For anything else, he would shrug and pronounce, "You get sick, you get well!"

I was in seventh grade when I believe my mother suffered a miscarriage. We were living in yet another small house, this time north of Benton. While I was watching my younger brothers I overheard my mother say to Aunt Ruby, "A shoe box will be big enough." They never discussed it further but my father quietly buried the box in a nearby field. It remained a private matter between my parents involving neither doctors nor the reporting of it to authorities. My mother recovered and three years later when she was 34 she gave birth to her final child. For whatever reasons, she let me name the baby. I was crazy about a boy who played the drums whose name was Billy Bob.

Reg and Joe Aaron.

As a large family we survived in no small part by depending on government subsistence, bartering and relying on relatives. During World War II the government gave out ration cards, good for sugar, coffee, gas and even tires. My mother and Aunt Ruby would swap cards, depending on what supplies the other needed. Uncle Joe would give the boys haircuts while Aunt Ruby, mother to three boys herself (Billy Gene, Lavern, and Bobby Joe, in order of birth), handed over clothes her own sons had outgrown. The county would occasion-

ally bring in free clothing, allowing the public a limit of two items per person. Three of my brothers were the same size so by swapping they could have six different shirts between them. I received two dresses and when I went to school every girl whose family was on relief was wearing my dress. Through the WPA (Works Progress Administration) my father and uncle Reg worked on the roads digging ditches.

* * * * * * * * *

When my father moved the remaining family to the Quad-Cities in the mid-1940s— some of us had left home already— his big-

Lawrence Edward, Billy Bob and Donald Eugene pictured in front of the "chicken house" in Castle Junction, Illinois.

gest hurdle was finding a landlord willing to rent to someone with so many children. Fortunately, a woman named Ethel Shroder and my father had mutual friends. She owned a motel off Route 67 in Castle Junction that had two adjacent houses with several cabins and a large chicken house. Although all of the prop-

erties were occupied the chicken house was empty. It was agreed that my father could move the family into the chicken house until one of the other properties became vacant. It was scoured clean, curtains were hung as room dividers, and soon the family settled in with the boys attending school in nearby Sherrard, Illinois.

With my brothers growing up and leaving home, my parents moved several years later to a two-story house off Seventh Street in Moline, Illinois. My father ran a local service station and one summer Aunt Ruby sent Billy Gene to help. My mother welcomed him as she loved being surrounded by family.

My parents eventually settled in Matherville, a small community 20 miles south of the Quad-Cities. My father

Josie Gulley and Billy Gene Aaron in front of the service station in Moline, Illinois.

would make the daily commute into Rock Island to his job at the R.E. Roth Co. where he would lose his life in an industrial accident, leaving my mother a widow at 53.

* * * * * * * * *

After my father's death my mother chose to remain in Matherville. My brother Bobby and his family lived on the opposite side of town. While spending the night with my mother Bobby's daughter Cindy noticed a large lump over my mother's left breast. Although she assured Cindy it was nothing and suggested it would probably go away, Cindy ignored her grandmother's indifference—this was the woman who lived her whole life by the credo "You get sick, you get well"—and told her parents. After a frantic discussion with Bobby and his wife Donna the next day, it was agreed my mother would visit Dr. Hastings in nearby Aledo. After some tests and a biopsy, Dr. Hastings determined it was cancer and ordered surgery. The procedure to remove my mother's left breast was performed at Mercer County Hospital. Post-operation, she was placed in a ward with four other women in a space so small you could barely squeeze between the beds.

After she was released Dr. Hastings set up 18 out-patient radiation treatments. My mother took them all, her chest resembling a severe sunburn after each session. Medicare paid her expenses. Upon her recovery we took her on a vacation back to

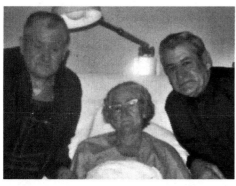

Thompsonville where she was reunited with Aunt Ruby and many of her friends that she knew throughout the area.

Although she enjoyed good health for the next few years we all noticed when she began coughing up phlegm and suffering from a lack of energy. I urged her to move in with us—in the back of our minds we knew the cancer had come back. Dr. Hastings confirmed that the cancer had returned and spread

Brothers Rex and Joe Aaron with Josie Gulley at the hospital in Aledo, Illinois near the end of her life.

to her lungs. We checked her into Mercer County Hospital but further surgery was not advised.

We took rotating shifts to be with her. She was alert most of the time but when she would wonder why she wasn't getting better I would lie to her, blaming her condition on a stubborn case of pneumonia. She must have questioned that diagnosis, especially when relatives living hundreds of miles away began arriving at her bedside—Aunt

Ruby and Uncle Joe and even her oldest brother Rex, who seldom left his home in Benton.

I wasn't with her the morning she died. My brother Lawrence Edward was in our kitchen and took the call from the hospital informing us she had passed away. The date was Feb. 4, 1972. We were all heartbroken even though we knew her cancer was terminal and it was merely a matter of time.

My mother left no will but it was decided amongst my brothers that I would be executor of the estate. We hired a Silvis attorney named McGehee who went with me to appear before a Mercer County judge because my mother had lived and died in Mercer County.

Before selling my mother's home we had to clear it out. There were scores of empty shoe boxes and wrapping paper piled high in the living room that we burned in the back yard. We gave away furniture to any of the grandchildren needing it. My brother Lawrence Edward was upset by the whole process, lamenting that we were "throwing all of her stuff away."

The house sold for $4,000 to Donna Gulley's brother, Larry Harris, who paid in cash. The money was placed in an account at the Uptown Bank in Moline out of which I paid her funeral expenses, her remaining doctor bills plus the obituary notices published in the area newspapers.

After a grace period of 10 months I closed the account and distributed the remaining money among my brothers who each received $304.28. The attorney was paid $572.00. The estate was formally closed Aug. 9, 1973.

My darling mother
In such a state
She loved you Lord
Why grant her this fate
She never drank, she never smoked
She looks so pitiful
Her will is broke
She looks so weak
And sick and frail
I cry and cry
To no avail
Lord, be gentle
If she must go
And love her dearly
For I did so

(Written by Bobby Gulley while at the bedside of his mother, days before her passing.)

Mable Gulley, age 12

2

THE BUCKET WAS ALWAYS FULL

Mable Gulley-Harvey

During the Great Depression we moved often around Franklin, Hamilton, and Saline counties in southern Illinois, ending up wherever my father could find work. It was not easy talking a landlord into renting to a family of nine. By 1937 we were living in Benton in a four-room house by the railroad tracks, two blocks from an old flour mill.

We had coal-burning stoves for heat—one in the living room, the other in the kitchen. Still, during the winter, the bedrooms were always freezing cold. The kitchen stove had an attached hot-water reservoir from which we would draw water for washing dishes and bathing. There was no indoor plumbing or basins—we drank well water from a bucket with a dipper, rinsed dishes in a pan, and the commode was a backyard outhouse with the Sears catalog in lieu of store-bought toilet paper.

Our bath was a round metal tub that barely accommodated one person. Shielding me from my leering brothers, my mother would stand guard by the kitchen door as I stripped and squeezed in, my knees up to my chin. My brothers would share my secondhand bathwater, reheating it after each use with more trips to the kitchen reservoir.

The Orient Coal Co. was doing business nearby so empty coal-hauling trains would rumble past pulling open box cars. They'd return loaded to overflowing with coal, inching by our place before gathering speed down the line. The locals nicknamed these slow-moving trains "coal drags".

With no money and a large family to support, my father, along with some of our neighbors—most no better off than we were—would steal coal. As the train crept by they would climb the ladders that ran up the sides and fling coal from the open box cars. Balancing on top, my father would ride two or three miles until the train started moving faster and he had to jump off and walk back home. After dark, he would return with his flashlight and wheel barrow to retrieve what he had thrown off, stashing the ill-gotten coal in the shed or under a lumber pile in case an official from the railroad happened by.

Once we'd burned through the coal supply my father would send us over to the railroad tracks with a bucket to pick through the dirt and weeds for any stray coal residue. "Don't come back unless the bucket is full," he'd threaten.

A volatile man, he wasn't above using a belt on his kids. Consequently, when he told us to do something, we did it, no questions asked. The bucket was always full.

Proud father Robert Harvey Sr. poses on the front porch with his firstborn, Robert Harvey Jr.

THOMPSONVILLE AND THE WAR YEARS

Mable Gulley-Harvey

My husband was born July 5, 1926, to Robert Earl Harvey Sr. and Jessie (White) Harvey in Thompsonville, Illinois.

The eldest of two boys—his brother William Joseph Harvey would be born two and a half years later—Robert (or Bob as I've always called him) was named after his father, although with his dark, gaunt features and slight bone structure (he would struggle his whole life finding shoes that fit), he more closely resembled his petite mother's side of the family while his brother inherited the stocky frame of his father.

His parents were active members of the Thompsonville Baptist Church and the brothers were raised with a strong Baptist presence in their lives. William (or more casually, Bill) chose to remain in Thompsonville his entire life and would eventually rise to the office of church deacon while Bob jettisoned most of the formalities of church and religion in general upon leaving the area.

Bob's habit of referring to his mother as "Mother" and grandmother as "Mom" was very confusing to me at first until I figured out that he was talking about two different women. Mom—I called her Miss White—doted on Bob, making his lunch daily while he attended school across the road. A

First day of school, Robert Harvey Jr.

Bess White

reluctant student, he favored arriving in the nick of time and leaving early when possible. Along with his mother and Aunt Helen (Jessie's sister), the women disciplined the boys while their father was away much of the time through the Great Depression years working as a prison guard at Menard in Chester, Illinois and for the Civilian Conservation Corps (CCC), the latter a public-relief program for the unemployed that was part of President Roosevelt's New Deal.

Bob's grandfather Joe White owned and operated the local feed store and gas station. A fanatical pinochle player he would game with his friends in the afternoons, pausing only to service customers before returning to the hand in progress. By age 11, Bob was helping his grandfather mix the various blends of feed, dumping wheat, barley, corn and oats on the floor and sifting it with shovels into brightly pat-terned 100-pound cotton feed sacks. Once empty, the locals often utilized the cotton bags to make dresses and aprons. Customers sometimes would favor particular bags for specif-ic patterns leaving Bob to unstack the entire pile if they liked one positioned on the bottom.

Joe White

Because he lost $800 to the Bank of Thompsonville during the Crash of 1929, Joe White distrusted banks, choosing instead to stash the proceeds from his businesses among the feed bags in his store. Bob and his friends often would discover the cash to the bemusement of his grandfather who would simply take the money from the boys

Robert Harvey Sr. inside his feed store. Note the colorful bags of grain which locals often used for dress material.

and find a new hiding place.

Although Bob had a talent for music—he played clarinet with his high-school band—his real passion was mechanics. After school each day he would head to the local garage run by Nick Droit and help work on cars. He received no pay but learned invaluable hands-on ex-perience. (After returning home from the Army, Bob would purchase his first automobile from Droit, a stripped-down 1934 Chevrolet. He later refurbished the car on his own after Droit balked at helping him piece it back together.)

In an era when turn signals were still considered optional, a local coal miner named Johnny Fizel installed a homemade set on his own vehicle, an accomplishment that drew

Bob to seek out the budding inventor. One of Thompsonville's quirky-but-brilliant characters (and an avid subscriber to the magazines "Popular Science" and "Mechanics Illustrated"), Fizel hand-built a generator for his farm and with Bob's assistance successfully designed and tested a diving helmet made from a water tank and a bicycle-tire pump.

Perhaps because of a personality clash with his own father Bob tended to gravitate toward older men in town who could serve as mentors (years later, his mother would lament not helping him as much as his younger brother Bill, who received both college funding from his parents and assistance

Robert Harvey Sr. in his prison guard uniform.

establishing his veterinary practice).

When he saw his uncle Roy Ing (Thompsonville's sole barber) race around town on his own homemade motorbike, Bob decided to design one himself. He removed the pedals from a bicycle, bolted down a platform for the engine—cobbled together from a washing machine motor—and welded an anti-freeze can to the frame for a gas tank. Installing a flywheel with a rope for a primitive starter, he fired the contraption up like a lawnmower. The machine would serve him well until he left for the Army.

Once Bob got his driver's license, his mother granted him permission to take his paternal grandfather Amos Calhoun Harvey to Evansville, Indiana, to watch the professional wrestling matches (Vern Gagne was a favorite). Driving more than 60 miles away from Thompsonville, Bob's mother seldom

Homemade motorbike designed and built by a teenage Robert Harvey Jr.

questioned the wisdom of letting a teenager (and his friends on occasion—Bob's grandfather often bought all of them tickets and snacks) undertake such a distant journey on school nights.

When Joe White died, Bob's father purchased the feed store and gas station from Joe's widow, Miss White. Bob worked selling ice for his father, driving the eight miles into Benton to pick up a load and then running a delivery route throughout the county to a host of businesses and homes.

Between Benton and Thompsonville was a roadhouse called Pickle City. Calm by day when Bob would make his ice deliveries, at night the place was rife with drunken patrons and prostitutes, the latter based out of a stone-and-glass building across the highway that the locals nicknamed the Pony Stables because it resembled a series of horse stalls. Outside the city limits, the police—perhaps being paid off by the owners—turned a blind eye to the nefarious activities taking place nightly (the roadhouse burned down years ago but the stalls where customers could enjoy a few moments of pre-paid carnal intimacy still stand, albeit weed-infested and abandoned).

Tired of his job and needing to earn what he termed "real" money Bob and his friend Jack Archer took off one summer to St. Louis. Staying at the YMCA the youths found employment loading trucks at a warehouse. Unfortunately for them, the job was across the bridge in East St. Louis so, minus a car, they were charged a toll of 5¢ to make the walk. They were so broke they took to stealing change from a newspaper vending machine. The two held out for three weeks before returning to Thompsonville.

Bob and another friend named Jimmy Elimon—he would become Thompsonville's next long-time barber—finished the summer by heading to the Ford Motor Co. factory in Hegewisch, just outside of Gary, Indiana. Bob installed instrument panels on the assembly line until returning to Thompsonville in time for his last year of high school.

* * * * * * * * *

Upon graduation, with World War II entering its final stages, Bob and Jimmy decided to volunteer for the Navy, signing up at the nearest recruitment center in Marion, Illinois. His physical revealed that Bob was color blind and unable to distinguish differences in hues, crucial to reading semaphore signals. While Jimmy was accepted and sent to the Naval Training Station in Chicago, Bob returned to Thompsonville where he was drafted into the Army and sent to Texas for six weeks of basic training, followed by a further stint in California, and finally a return trip back to Texas for advance training (like many young volunteers and recruits, Bob was 17 when he joined the military but as per government decree, no young man under the age of 18 could be shipped off to war).

Pvt. Robert E. Harvey Jr.

In due time during 1945, Bob joined his fellow draftees on a slow-moving troop ship headed for the Philippine Islands where a staging area for replacement soldiers had been established. En route, news reached the ship that in the aftermath of the nuclear bombings of Hiroshima Aug. 6 and Nagasaki Aug. 9, Japan had announced its surrender Aug. 15. On Sept. 2, officials of the Japanese government signed the Japanese Instrument of Surrender—the war was over.

Victory celebrations broke out on board—the young men naively assumed they would all return home immediately—but the ship continued its course, first to Manila and then Leyte Island, where living quarters in the form of newly erected tents awaited the soldiers. Bob noted they had wooden floors, giving the new arrivals a reprieve from the tropical mud. Meanwhile, B-52 bombers dispatched from Bob's base continued their air assaults on some of the more remote islands where many Japanese soldiers carried on fighting despite their country's official surrender.

Boarding a tank landing ship, Bob was taken to Kyoto, Japan, where he was assigned to the 6th Army Administration office. Kyoto, the oldest city in Japan, had been spared from Allied bombing. Bob rode the street cars and enjoyed the sights until the 6th Army Administration was disbanded and he was reassigned to the Civil Information and Education office in Tokyo. In the Radio Tokyo Building (a bastion of broadcasting before the war), Bob worked as a clerk typist, sharing space with 12 other assignees and several interpreters. He and the others slept five to a room in the Finance Building, mere blocks from General Douglas MacArthur's headquarters in the Daiichi Building.

Bob held the rank of corporal and therefore was barred from using the motor pool so he would seek out sergeants willing to sign out a Jeep. He and his friends would tour the city and surrounding area. Tokyo had no gas stations so they would fill five-gallon cans with fuel for their journeys.

One of the more memorable highlights for the young men was touring Mount Fujiyama, an extinct volcano in the central part of Japan. At 12,395 feet high, Bob felt as though he were walking up a very steep hill. They counted 10 shacks along the route where he and the others would duck in out of the cold and build fires in the grates to brew green tea. They made their way to the side of the mountain where the Shinto Shrine is nestled just above the clouds. Taking photographs the entire way Bob realized he had dropped part of his camera somewhere along the path but was too tired to retrace his steps.

* * * * * * * * *

HEADQUARTERS SIXTH ARMY
Office of the Ordnance Officer

25 November 1945

CERTIFICATE

As his Commanding Officer, I certify that Pvt. Robert E. Harvey, ASN 36929463,
is authorized to retain in his possession the following item of legally obtained
captured enemy material: One Carbine with Bayonet.

PHILIP G. BLACKMORE,
Brigadier General, United States Army,
Ordnance Officer.

Official permission allowing Pvt. Robert E. Harvey to ship home his "spoils of war."

With all the exotic sights and sounds preoccupying his days and nights Bob didn't realize that his mother back in Thompsonville hadn't heard from him in weeks. She went through various military channels until she reached the chaplain of Bob's unit. Called before the clergyman, Bob received a lecture about the importance of maintaining contact with your loved ones back home during wartime. Duly chastened, he began flooding the mail with photographs and gifts—beautiful silk tablecloths and napkins, a porcelain tea set and five saddles to his brother Bill and cousin Jerry Cook, who owned Shetland ponies. Even though it required special permission, he also sent along several Japanese rifles.

Robert Harvey Jr. (left) stationed in Japan with two of his army buddies.

As their time overseas rapidly wound down Bob spent most of his days filling out forms for the men in his unit who were going home. The last to leave, he filed his own release papers and found a general to sign him out. His final work as clerk typist for the Army involved laying out the troop ship's newsletter while it was en route to the United States.

Docking in San Diego, he boarded a train to Fort Sheridan, Illinois, where he was formally discharged from the Army Nov. 11, 1946. He was given $16.20 for his bus ticket back to Thompsonville and his final "mustering out" check from the military amounted to $352.80.

Glad to be back in his hometown among family and friends the ever-frugal ex-recruit collected the cash he had sent back to his mother and promptly purchased a car from Nick Droit. He rejoined the Thompsonville Baptist Church and pondered his next move. What it would be, he didn't know, but to a young man who had seen the world in all its beauty and brutality there had to be more to life beyond the city limits of Thompsonville, Illinois, population 568.

DOC HARVEY

Brad Harvey

There was a brief period when my parents considered moving back to Thompsonville for their retirement. We spent a few days one summer building a garage but plans changed and the property was sold to my grandparents' former neighbors, the Isaacs.

My father had inherited the massive brick building that once had housed my grandfather's feed store. With that business long gone—the frontage to this day still sports the black-and-yellow signage reading "Harvey's Feed Store"—my grandfather had derived an income from renting the rear of the building to the school system for their fleet of buses (when another tenant became erratic with his obligations—at one point missing two years' worth of rent payments—my parents found it easier to sell the building and all its inherent eviction issues to the Isaacs for the sum of $1,200).

The brick building was a target of vandals, but my father reduced the damage by covering up the large windows in front with plywood. The other pressing need was the seasonal upkeep of the roof, which required gallons of hot tar applied by mops and push brooms. Being 12 and possessing strong legs, I would run the buckets of tar up the ladder for my father.

On this occasion he had acquired a dozen barrels of tar from one of the locals. Stubborn and sticky, the liquid had jelled in the bottom of each container. So my father had built a fire under a platform of bricks to heat the residue tar and drain it from a plug on top of each barrel.

Because lunch remained a sacred rite, my father and his buddy left me in charge of the fire while they repaired down the road for a quick sandwich.

These particular barrels of tar had been stored outside, where the rain had seeped through the ill-fitting plugs on top, filling the containers with water. Now the fire was

The former Harvey's Feed Store in Thompsonville, Illinois.

boiling the contents of the barrel into a mixture of super-heated liquid that was spewing out of the opening and creating a pool of flaming tar that was rapidly expanding by the minute. The fire was out of control.

Twenty feet away and sharing the same lot as the former feed store was my Uncle Bill's veterinarian clinic. I ran through the back door of the clinic, found my uncle, and sputtered, "Fire! You'd better get out here quick and take a look!" I expected more of a reaction but my uncle very calmly stopped what he was doing, acknowledged my flustered presence, and calmly led the way back outside where the flames were now towering over us.

"Well," muttered my uncle with all the emotion of a man reaching for a salt shaker, "I guess I'd better call the fire department."

Within moments the Thompsonville Volunteer Fire Department arrived on the scene—as did seemingly the entire populace of the town to view the spectacle—and made short work of the conflagration. Congratulations flowed among the heroes of the day, and I took what was supposed to be a good-natured ribbing from a few of the bystanders over the spreading of a fire that was not my fault.

Once the crowd had dispersed, my uncle went back inside his veterinarian clinic. I was amazed that despite the urgency of the moment when disaster could have razed his livelihood my uncle's demeanor remained calm and detached.

* * * * * * * * *

While my father enjoyed a perfunctory relationship with the public school system—a pattern I copied throughout my own adolescence—his younger brother Bill

William Harvey
(college photo)

would embrace it. After completing high school in 1945, Bill entered Southern Illinois University of Carbondale and graduated with a degree in agriculture in 1949 with an aim toward teaching. Finding his easy-going temperament ill-suited when it came to meting discipline to unruly students—complicated by a hearing loss dating back to childhood—he put his teaching plans on hold and entered the United States Air Force, serving in the Korean War as a medic and meat inspector. His commanding officer was Captain Frederick B. Clooney, the base veterinarian, and his influence determined Bill's new career path. After discharge from the Air Force, he entered the University of Illinois and graduated in 1960 with a degree in veterinary medicine. Bill would set up practice and spend the next 53 years servicing Thompsonville and its surrounding communities.

As a sheltered city kid fond of animals I found my uncle's occupation alternately fascinating and horrifying. At my first livestock auction I watched wranglers kick at squealing piglets while they herded them through a series of pens. Once they had a terrified beast cornered they would grab its hind legs and hold it up so my uncle could inoculate it. He would squeeze its testicles and proceed to slice the scrotum off with a blade, tossing the bloody sac onto an ever-growing pile that would be a foot high by the end of the day. This was to prevent what was called "Boar's Taint," an unpleasant odor caused by pheromones produced by sexually mature animals that would affect the smell and taste of slaughtered pork.

For this my uncle would earn 50¢ per pig. And I would learn that people who enjoy bacon shouldn't see it being made.

When an animal was too large or sick to be removed from a barn or field my uncle would treat it on site. I was with him when a sow big enough to inflict grievous bodily harm to a human suddenly scrambled to its feet and began chasing us. We dove for safety over the electric fence while the enraged swine paced back and forth, snorting its displeasure at having its personal space invaded.

Airman William Harvey

Of course he treated his share of dogs and cats. He risked being bitten, scratched or defecated on each time he hoisted someone's squirming pet onto his steel examination table, its claws slipping and sliding across the shiny surface while he tried to administer treatment. His opinions waivered over whether he preferred dealing with larger animals like horses whose kick could maim or getting nipped by an elderly person's lap dog.

There was never any doubt regarding my uncle's moral character and commitment to the town he'd called home his entire life. He was ordained as a deacon in 1965 and served as a Sunday school teacher for 50 years. He belonged to both the high school and village boards and helped organize the Thompsonville Volunteer Fire Department. When my great uncle Opal died in office, Bill stepped in until a replacement mayor was found.

* * * * * * * * *

I always had hobbies that drew derision from some of the locals, be it comic books or later on, music, specifically the Beatles. For years I was told one of the group had a sister that lived in the area. I wrote the notion off as another joke made at my expense. Thompsonville in those days resembled Hooterville, the fictional small town in the television show "Green Acres." Although no one had to climb a power pole to answer their telephone, a cynic couldn't help but notice similar archetypes shared by both. How could the sibling of a global phenomenon end up in such an isolated backwater as Franklin County, Illinois?

Louise Harrison had arrived in Benton in 1963 with her husband, a highly paid engineer employed by a West Frankfort mining company, and two small children. In September of 1963, while the Beatles were consolidating their success across Great Britain and the rest of Europe, the group took a short sabbatical. George Harrison, with older brother Peter in tow, decided to visit their sister in America (many Beatles books erroneously report Louise as living in St. Louis). George played with a local group called the Four Vests at a VFW hall in Eldorado (the first performance by a Beatle on American soil), picked up the original album by James Ray containing George's future cover hit "Got My Mind Set on You" at Barton and Collins (a Benton department store on the town square), and bought a Rickenbacker guitar from a shop in Mt. Vernon.

In addition, Louise, acting as a self-appointed public relations flack for her brother's band, got George an interview on West Frankfort radio station WFRX, another first, while plugging the Beatles' version of "From Me to You" over the hit version sung by Del Shannon. The locals considered Louise's brother a polite eccentric with a funny haircut while scarcely believing the tales of his band's popularity overseas—at least until Feb. 9, 1964, when they along with a record 73 million television viewers saw the phenomenon firsthand on the Ed Sullivan show.

Although Louise would leave the area, she returned for a time to a small village outside Thompsonville called Macedonia. Bill took care of her animals and Louise, probably relieved to be spared regurgitating stories about her famous brother for the nth time, regaled my history-loving uncle with tales of growing up in Liverpool during the German bombing raids of World War II. When George contracted the cancer that would eventually claim his life, my uncle approached Louise and offered to put her brother's name on the church's prayer list.

* * * * * * * * *

The love of my uncle's life, Ruth Clark was born Dec. 7, 1941 to Gladys and Roffie Clark, who owned a farm just outside Thompsonville. From the day of his daughter's birth Roffie had determined that Ruth would one day grow up and marry Thompsonville's most eligible bachelor (my grandmother Jessie held the baby shower for Ruth's mother, sealing the deal). An extrovert with energy to burn, Ruth would help bring the reticent veterinarian out of his shell, becoming the proverbial woman be-

Dr. and Mrs. William Harvey, wedding day, June 27, 1965.

hind the man. They wed on June 27, 1965.

Between my Uncle Bill's salary as the region's preeminent animal doctor and my Aunt Ruth's tenure at the West Frankfort Bank (now the Banterra Bank), they lived well but never ostentatiously, which isn't to say they didn't enjoy their hobbies. They gave to their church, formed several outside businesses together and collected vintage automobiles, owning 15 at one count. When my mother and father divested themselves of all remaining property in Thompsonville, they traded their former home and adjacent land to Bill and Ruth for an antique rocking chair and a 1956 Oldsmobile.

"Doc" Harvey with wife Ruth.

For years my aunt and uncle remained Thompsonville's unofficial goodwill ambassadors, always a fixture at sporting events and area functions.

As he entered his fifth decade as DVM Bill began to experience health issues, suffering several heart attacks and enduring open heart surgery. He maintained regular office hours until May 16, 2012, when he confessed to Ruth that he was tired of it all. He died eight days later on May 24 from an aneurism in the bottom of his heart. He was 83.

Born and raised a farm girl, Ruth still keeps bees and chickens, offering those who visit eggs and honey when available. Of her generation, she's the last living link between the past and present Thompsonville. She notes that Bill would not be happy with some of the changes to the town, pointing to the new liquor store recently opened just around the curve from Bill's former veterinarian clinic.

"If Bill were still alive, that business would not be here," she assures me.

* * * * * * * * *

The people of Thompsonville chose to remember the man they called "Doc" Harvey by naming the high school gymnasium in his honor, with a plaque prominently displayed in the gym lobby.

School Board President Leon McClerren told the Franklin County News, "Doc was a pillar of this community forever. He did what he did, not to be recognized but to make Thompsonville a better place to live, work and attend school. He took care of people's pets and if they could pay it was fine and if they couldn't pay it was fine. He did it all without fanfare. He really cared about Thompsonville."

School photo of Joseph Charles Gulley taken in Galatia, Illinois.
(Photo courtesy of Christopher Gulley)

5

CHARLES WE HARDLY KNEW YE

Brad Harvey

Joseph Charles Gulley was the oldest of six boys and like many big brothers felt the weight of expectations throughout his life.

Born on February 5, 1930 in Benton, Illinois, he was named after his Uncle Joe and paternal grandfather Charles "Shorty" Gulley. While an adolescent—in keeping with the Gulley boys' tradition of near-fatal accidents—he tumbled out of a barn loft, catching his throat on a protruding nail and narrowly missed his jugular vein. An uneven hovel built into a steep hillside, the barn was the type of dangerous structure that only people of limited means such as the Gulleys would ever consider inhabiting.

Pulled out of high school while only 17, Charles and his younger brother Bobby accompanied their father north to the Quad-Cities, where they were told to lie about their ages in order to land lucrative factory jobs at the J.I. Case plant in Bettendorf, Iowa. Charles would later follow his father to the Roy E. Roth factory where he became a spot welder, making gasoline tanks for use in tractors and other farm-related machinery.

* * * * * * * * *

In the 1950s being drafted and sent to Korea—officially a "police action" and not a war—was foremost in the minds of most able-bodied young men. Charles mistakenly sought to avoid the draft by signing on with the Illinois National Guard, who, to his chagrin, soon were activated and deployed overseas.

Irene Nesseler would often make the walk from her Rock Island home on 11th street and 18th avenue to the Prom, a roller skating rink atop the hill on Brady Street, across the river in Davenport, Iowa. On this particular occasion a fight with a suitor left an opportunity for Charles, who was instantly smitten with the pretty, dark-haired girl. He offered her a ride home. With thoughts of Korea and his imminent deployment weighing heavily, Charles and Irene married in haste Sept. 10, 1950.

Irene Nesseler. (Photo courtesy of Christopher Gulley)

Luckily for Charles, his two years in the service left him unscathed. He learned to cut hair (a skill he applied on me and his future sons around the kitchen table), saw Marilyn Monroe entertain the troops and at one point borrowed a jeep to visit his brother-in-law Bill Harvey, also serving.

Charles wrote home advising his mother on the various clothing sizes for his new bride (36" blouse, 18" slip) and voicing concerns that "Rene"—his nickname

for Irene—had her automobile sufficiently "all fixed up for the winter." He commiserated with his mother over some undisclosed ailment troubling his father, adding "I hope daddy is ok now. I guess he is working too hard. He is like his son, he's not built for hard work." It might have been Charles' first acknowledgement to his parents that he held loftier ambitions than toiling away in the Quad-Cities factories (during his military service Charles would earn the Bronze Service Star, his Korean Service and United Nations Service medals).

Once back from overseas Charles slipped uneasily into his role as family man and chief provider. Like many young married women Irene craved security and if Charles harbored any

Joseph Charles Gulley in Korea.

creative dreams at this juncture he put them aside to earn a living—it was an era when men were expected to be stoic and support their families without question. He found a job doing auto body repair, breathing in noxious paint fumes as he welded and hammered disabused fenders and bumpers. He purchased a modest home in Rock Island. With the birth of their first child, Brian David Gulley, on March 6, 1956, married life for Charles and Irene seemed picture-perfect.

* * * * * * * * *

"Come see our new son!"

Charles' pronouncement that he and Irene had adopted came as an unexpected shock to his siblings. More than 50 years later the details surrounding the June 1964 arrival of Christopher Allen Gulley into the family remain shrouded in mys-

tery. Neither Irene nor Charles ever spoke at length about it during their lifetimes. "Charles told so many stories, you never knew what to believe," commented my mother, noting her eldest brother's penchant for zealously guarding his personal life.

As the baby grew older and began exhibiting certain physical traits—specifically the jug-ears which act as a Gulley genetic watermark—his paternity became harder for Charles to repudiate. Allegedly the result of a tryst with a married office worker whose husband was stationed overseas, Charles arranged a hurried

Joseph Charles, Irene and Brian welcome Christopher Allen into the Gulley family. (Photo courtesy of Christopher Gulley)

adoption through a Davenport attorney. The baby was apparently "handed off" in a parking lot. One has to wonder what sort of conversation passed between husband and wife regarding this sudden addition to the family—it's doubtful Irene was oblivious to the baby's origins—but nevertheless, she grew to love the child. Brian was studying Christopher Columbus at his grade school and got the honor of naming his new baby brother.

The adoption was not as seamless as it appeared. It was rumored that Christopher's birth mother had on occasion stalked both Charles and Irene. In another odd twist Christopher recalls an obsessive Irene driving him and his brother to the Moline home of a woman—he remembers her last name as Johns—and parking on a side street while a reluctant Brian, at Irene's urging, peered through the windows of the house. Whether Johns was the elusive birth mother or simply another of Charles' flings, my own mother firmly believes that Irene knew the full details of Christopher's parentage.

* * * * * * * * *

Charles was adept at compartmentalizing the baser aspects of his life. He would swap automobiles with his younger brother Lawrence Edward as a smokescreen, and continued seeing other women. Lawrence Edward was the first to call attention to

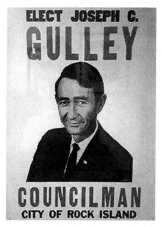

ELECT JOSEPH C.
GULLEY
COUNCILMAN
CITY OF ROCK ISLAND

(Courtesy of Christopher Gulley)

his brother's escalating alcohol problem, recounting a drunken incident on the grounds of the Plantation (an upscale restaurant in Moline) when the two of them tussled over the affections of the female piano player. So convincing was Charles at controlling his self-image few believed there was a darker side to his personality.

He loved to sketch and had an appreciation for the dramatic arts, something Christopher recognized when he watched his father emcee a local presentation of "Fractured Follies" for the Policeman's Benevolent Association (both Brian and Christopher, in particular, would go on to become active in theater). Charles befriended Jim Shaw, a former Rock Island County sheriff who served as county coroner from 1964-1977. Breathing the rarified air of local politics vicariously through Shaw, Charles ran for Rock Island City Council under the campaign slogan "By Gulley, By Golly!" and lost. Christopher believed that this was Charles' great last attempt at aspiring to something beyond the nine-to-five that had ruled his life since he had been a teenager lying about his age to gain entry into the area shops.

Given the destructive undercurrents coursing through the marriage it was inevitable that Charles and Irene would divorce. Both Brian and Christopher were caught in the middle as their parents argued over money and custody issues. Charles left the area, relocating to Waterloo, Iowa, where he worked as a claims adjuster. He met his second wife Annemarie, a hostess for a local hotel, and the two would move to Casper, Wyoming, ultimately settling in Campbell, California, where they became property managers. Essentially her sons' sole means of support, Irene took a job with Bituminous Casualty, a position she held for 35 years. She never remarried.

* * * * * * * * *

Brian was sick. Never a robust individual, he looked positively skeletal when he showed up for a Gulley family reunion in 1988, using a walker to steady his gait. Our aunt Donna Gulley notified Christopher, then serving in the Navy, about Brian's shocking condition.

Last photo taken of Christopher and Brian together before Brian's untimely death from AIDS. (Photo courtesy of Christopher Gulley)

He was unprepared for the sight that greeted him upon arriving at Brian's San Francisco apartment. Though the brothers bantered and joked as they had in the past, Christopher knew he was witnessing a dead man walking. Meanwhile Irene, always a nervous flyer, chose to take the train to California to see her ailing son.

Brian would soon pass away due to complications from AIDs. Given the social stigma of the disease—public attention remained fixated on the homosexual connotations despite it being an equal opportunity ravager—Irene seemed unable to accept the official cause of death, suggesting it was cancer or a brain tumor as if in denial of Brian's true sexual orientation. He was cremated and his ashes were returned to Rock Island for interment. He was 32.

* * * * * * * * *

Charles cut himself off from the family once he left the Quad-Cities. Brian would live with him briefly in Casper, storming out after a misunderstanding over his accommodations. My mother lent Christopher money to see Charles upon his graduation from high school. Wishing to avoid an unpleasant scene given his mother's antipathy toward his father, Christopher left for Casper without telling Irene. She responded by calling the police in Wyoming, accusing Charles of kidnapping. For Irene, the psychological wounds inflicted during her marriage would never quite heal.

My mother, along with brothers Bobby, Billy and Don, traveled out to visit Charles at various times. What they found was a man they no longer knew. They remained silent as Charles introduced them to friends and colleagues as captains of industry and

corporate hog farmers, not sure if Charles was joking or ashamed of his Midwestern siblings. My mother thought Charles was resentful over the success that had visited his younger brothers but eluded him as the eldest. He confirmed to her one nagging suspicion: Christopher was his biological son.

Christopher had made several attempts to establish a bond with his long-distance father. He poured out his feelings in a Father's Day card, admitting that like his brother, he too was gay. When Charles finally did re-

Mable Gulley-Harvey during a rare visit with Joseph Charles in his later years.

spond it was with a photo of father and son taken at Black Hawk State Historic Site many years ago in which he scrawled a message on the back informing Christopher that he loved him.

Charles told Annemarie that he was afraid he would die young like his father, killed at age 53 in an industrial accident. He was 57 and struggling with throat cancer as well as a drinking problem that he never resolved. He desperately missed his boys and spoke of them often.

He passed away on Nov. 11, 1987 from a massive heart attack, mere months before Brian's death. Within a year Christopher had lost half of his family. Irene would die in an assisted living center Jan. 30, 2018 at age 86.

Christopher made sporadic efforts to access his adoption records but his interest in knowing the details surrounding his birth has waned over the years. In middle-age he can recognize the foibles of his parents—the unfaithful father who nonetheless risked all to keep his son and the self-sacrificing mother willing to accept another's child as her own.

A parting shot: In a scrawled note on the back of this photo Joseph Charles revealed his true feelings for adopted son Christopher. (Photo courtesy of Christopher Gulley)

Modene Pogue (right) and her mother sit with baby Jill Harvey.

NUMBER PLEASE?

Mable Gulley-Harvey

My first job was housekeeping for Everett and Villa Carlisle, owners of the local grocery store in Thompsonville. Two hours a week I would dust and run the vacuum, earning 35 cents an hour plus all the candy bars I could sneak from their kitchen cupboard.

After graduating from high school in 1946 I applied as a switchboard operator at the telephone company in Benton. I lived eight miles away but didn't drive, so I resolved my commuter issues by temporarily moving in with my Aunt Ruby in West City.

My friend Modene Pogue, another new graduate, was unemployed and living with her widowed mother. After persuading her to work at the telephone company with me, we found a place together in a house on North Main Street off the town square within walking distance to our jobs.

The landlady, whose husband was gone most of the time driving a bus for Greyhound, charged us $7 a week rent and would eyeball us as we crossed her living room to the stairs leading to our room. The only caveat was sharing a bathroom with another tenant, a mechanic who rode a motorcycle. With his leather jacket, skull cap and grimy appearance, Modene was afraid of him but he didn't bother me because I grew up with six brothers.

The telephone office was on the second floor of a four-story walk-up on the south side of the square. We scaled the creaking steps of the building daily but at night we were terrified as we always felt as if someone was approaching us from behind.

Our work area had a bank of six switchboards along the wall. We were given headsets along with 24 "sending" and "receiving" cords arranged into two rows of 12. When a caller picked up their receiver, it would trigger a light on the switchboard. We would plug in a "receiving" cord below, ask "Number please?", and connect them by plugging in a "sending" cord, activating the ringer manually by pulling on a key. If there was static, it meant the line was busy so we would inform the caller, pull out both cords and wait for the next light.

Modene Pogue and Mable Gulley-Harvey, old friends reunited.

It was slow at night so we would lock the office doors after 11 p.m. I worked local calls while another employee handled the more complicated long distance calls. By 3 a.m. I usually was left alone to watch the switchboards while the long distance operator napped in the break room. To stay awake I fortified myself nightly with Coca-Cola.

There was a taxi stand by the door of our building. The drivers worked day and night like we did and would keep an eye out when we walked home through the deserted square at night—even the bars closed by 2 a.m. We felt safe when the Greyhound bus would let off passengers at the nearby service station. Otherwise, we would dash past the post office and alley, ready to dodge any assailants lurking in the shadows until we arrived breathless at our front door.

I spent most of my paycheck on shoes. I had felt deprived owning one pair of penny loafers when I was in school. You could buy a pair of shoes for $2.98—the closet of our room was full of them. Modene, however, gave her widowed mother her money. She seemed to manage it better than I did.

I lasted a year at the job. The summer I quit I saw my future husband Robert Harvey Jr. for the first time.

Mable Gulley, 1946.

7

ARRESTED DEVELOPMENT

Mable Gulley-Harvey

On my weekends off from my switchboard job in Benton I would come back to Thompsonville to be with my family.

I was in the living room with my mother talking about my day while taking occasional glances out the window at my two little brothers, ages 5 and 7, while they played with their bright red coaster wagon on the sidewalk.

Our neighbor Pauline Fowler, 12, had wandered over. It occurred to me that she was too old to be playing with my brothers. After watching for a few minutes I realized she was trying to take their wagon. She kept grabbing the handle and pushing my brothers off the walk into the ditch next to the busy highway.

I stormed out of the house, approached Pauline and told her to leave the boys alone and go home. Defiant, she tightened her grip on the wagon handle and screeched, "I don't have to go home!"

Enraged, I drew my right arm back and swung at Pauline as hard as I could. But she was quick, dodging the blow by jumping backwards into the ditch and running away. It took her seconds to sprint across the vacant lot that separated her house from ours and disappear inside.

My brothers, amused by this uncommon display of temper in their 18-year-old sister, went back to playing.

A few days later my father was asked to come to the mayor's house with me in tow. Pauline had told her father that I had hit her on the legs and he in turn reported to the mayor that I had assaulted his daughter. I wasn't under arrest— Thompsonville had no police department—but I still had to appear and give my side of the story.

Pauline and I, with our fathers, sat opposite each other in the mayor's kitchen. A heavy-set man with a full head of white hair, the mayor nodded as Pauline explained how I had beaten her on the back of the legs with a stick and with great melodramatic flair raised her dress to show everyone the red marks.

Every time I stammered "You're lying!" during her bogus testimony my father would tell me to keep quiet. No one questioned what possible motive I would have in physically attacking Pauline. When finally allowed to speak, I proposed that Pauline had gotten the red marks from straddling her own wagon and that possibly before arriving she had spent the morning making her "injuries" look worse.

In the end, the mayor sided with Pauline and her father and levied a $50 fine against me. Begrudgingly, my father paid it in increments. Oddly, there was no paperwork generated over the matter. We used to joke about the mayor and Pauline's father sharing the money and giving Pauline a reward for being such a believable liar.

Joseph Charles, Donald Eugene and Bobby Gulley.

STILL WATERS

Brad Harvey

My Uncle Bobby was barely 16 when his father pulled both him and his older brother Charles out of high school, coached them on lying about their respective ages, and got the three of them jobs at the J. I. Case plant in Bettendorf, Iowa.

It was a move necessitated by economic hardship. With the rest of the Gulley family living hand-to-mouth in southern Illinois, my grandfather was desperate to take advantage of the well-paying jobs building farm machinery in the north. Although he valued education, the need for money circumvented all else. Subsequently, neither of his two sons would graduate high school and in the case of Bobby, the move would have near-fatal consequences.

Bobby's duties involved driving a fork-lift, shuttling loads of parts throughout the plant as needed. The vehicle was designed so that the operator would stand over the foot pedals that controlled the brake and accelerator. Gasoline-powered, they required removable fuel tanks that were stored away from the general work area. It was while racing another fork-lift to swap out fuel canisters that Bobby swerved to avoid a worker who stepped into his path. Slamming on the brake, the sudden stop threw Bobby to the pavement, his right leg taking full brunt of the impact. He was hospitalized and my mother recalled he was there long enough "to waste away to almost nothing."

Although the incident had happened on factory grounds and was work-related, there never was any question of suing the company. Bobby's age made the matter problematic legally plus his cousin Billy Gene Aaron and a friend named Woody Reed were similarly underage. Bobby feared in the event of a lawsuit they too would be scrutinized and lose their jobs that they needed as desperately as the Gulleys.

Bobby Gulley, Jim Mandrell and Joseph Charles Gulley. Mandrell was the first to move north and take advantage of the high-paying factory jobs.

Discharged from the hospital, Bobby spent nearly four months on crutches. His right leg was prone to infections and at one point it began to atrophy, contorting so badly the heel of his foot nearly touched his buttocks. A doctor named Myers thought the inflamed leg might be cancerous and should be amputated to save Bobby's life. My grandfather rejected the notion outright, claiming that if his son were to die, it would be with all of his body parts still attached. They found better luck with a second doctor named Sechter who kept Bobby under observation and dismissed any further suggestions of amputation.

Sufficiently recovered, Bobby found employment at the Rock Island Millworks building windows and doors, discovering a latent talent in carpentry. On the advice of my grandfather, he would secure a $500 loan and purchase a Rock Island home at auction, transporting it piece-by-piece to Matherville, where he would reassemble the structure on his own land. Bobby would construct two of his own houses and undertake boutique projects like assembling grandfather clocks, all without benefit of blueprints or schematics. His replica of city founder Col. George Davenport's house is displayed in the museum of the Rock Island Arsenal.

He met Donna Lee Harris through his sister-in-law Sally Gulley, the two women having been long-time friends. Uncommonly ambitious, Donna had grown up one of 13 siblings raised in unspeakable poverty by parents ill-equipped to handle the needs of their own children. They frequently were farmed out to neighbors and relatives when the parents became overwhelmed. Donna remembered how their father would often eat his meals elsewhere, bringing home leftover soybeans and grain gleaned from horse stalls and pig pens, leaving her and her hungry siblings to pick through the grist for something edible.

The poverty of the early years haunted Donna, who would spend the rest of her life distancing herself from those hardscrabble beginnings. She kept gardens, was an adept seamstress and, after gaining a government position at the Rock Island Arsenal (Bobby would join her later on), never missed an opportunity to advance her career.

She and Bobby married in April of 1953.

* * * * * * * * *

It was Bobby's new brother-in-law Wayne Jordan who introduced him to the guitar. Wayne led his own band and at his behest one Christmas,

Mr. and Mrs. Bobby Gulley.

Donna purchased a Gibson acoustic/electric guitar for Bobby. Jordan would exhort his brother-in-law to "keep strumming, don't quit!" whenever the novice guitarist would lag behind the beat. Bobby possessed a fine baritone singing voice similar to his younger brother Don. But the shy and retiring player would never equal Don's hog-calling intensity and extrovert nature when it came to performing.

Wayne and Dick Seales were two talented brothers who had been kicking around the Quad-Cities music scene for a number of years. They approached Bobby with an eye toward cutting a demo that would secure them all work at the local bars, offering Bobby a shot at fronting their new band. The trio adjourned to a small recording studio in Davenport, Iowa called Fredlo (a contraction of Fred and Lois Mauck, the couple who owned it) and within an hour had put down covers of "Jealous Heart" and "Afraid," two country western standards. Wayne's bass and Dick's lead guitar work borrowed heavily from Elvis sidemen Scotty Moore and Bill Black, while Bobby's melodic crooning—swathed in echo per the production values of the day—was confident and self-assured.

Several copies of the two-sided disc were pressed, but further collaborations between Bobby and the Seales were mooted by Donna, who feared the local night life offered temptations that her handsome, talented husband might not be able to resist. Wayne Seales would father two musical sons, Jim and Jack, who would experience success as members of the hit country act Shenandoah and the Moline-based Sweetwater Band, respectively. In 1994 I worked with Jack on the Christmas classic "Run, Run Rudolph," a recording that featured 21 Quad-Cities' area musicians. Tragically, Jack would take his own life in 2004, while his father Wayne died in 2006.

* * * * * * * * *

After 34 years—beating Bobby's 18—Donna retired from the Rock Island Arsenal. With her husband she had raised two successful children. Cindy would end up as a professor at Cornell University, while Steve became a carpenter and maintenance supervisor in his hometown of Matherville. Donna owned several comfortable homes, traveled, and gave freely of herself to her community and local charities. She had even conquered a chronic smoking habit by becoming a runner at age 50.

Donna had escaped the nightmare of an impoverished childhood but could not out-distance herself from the cancer that had already taken several of her siblings. She died Nov. 1, 2014, at age 80.

* * * * * * * * *

Always the soft-spoken Gulley brother, Bobby suffers from hearing loss, which can render him somewhat remote in conversations. Given his introverted nature and ready access to hearing aids, this may be a shy man's selective coping mechanism.

Minus Donna's kinetic energy, the house they once shared is oddly quiet, albeit modern and immaculate, betraying none of the clutter one associates with a man a few years shy of 90 and a great-grandparent.

Ask how he was able to build such intricate pieces like the grandfather clock in his living room without formal training or guidance, Bobby will offer a humble grin, tap the side of his head with an index finger and mutter, "It's all up here..."

*Lawrence Gulley checks out the concrete in their
newly-constructed home while Josie Gulley looks on.*

9

MYSTERY OF THE HOUSE FIRE

Mable Gulley-Harvey

My childhood was a blur of rental houses throughout Benton, Galatia and Cornerville—six in all including a 20-acre farm where we milked cows and sold the product to the local dairy.

By 1944 we inched closer to Thompsonville, moving to a four-room house outside the city limits near an overhead bridge. A big bay window faced the highway. In the winter we would amuse ourselves by watching cars slide down the steep, frozen road.

Franklin and the surrounding counties were dotted with oil wells. My father, always striving for something better, got a job with the oil company as a gauge reader, keeping tabs on the wells as they pumped oil into the attached reservoir tanks. After a few months of steady pay he was able to purchase a white two-story house with a partial basement inside the Thompsonville city limits.

There were three bedrooms and for the first time in my life one was mine. I relished the privacy even though I didn't have the right things to make it into a proper girl's bedroom. I was used to sleeping on living room couches or in the kitchen on a daybed, having to get up and crawl into my parents' queen-size at daybreak when my mother would come in to make my father's breakfast.

To keep the coal soot from dirtying our new living room my father opted to install the heating stove in the basement with a wooden grate over it to contain the ash. Unfortunately, this minor home improvement would have disastrous consequences.

My parents were driving me home from my job in Benton when the Benton Fire Department truck came roaring up behind and passed us, heading toward Thompsonville. Curious, my father began following and as we entered the city limits, to our horror we realized they were racing to our house. The place already was engulfed in flames and it seemed as though half the population of Thompsonville had come out to watch it burn. The fire department was unable to save it.

Lawrence Gulley astride a bicycle, one of the few possessions not destroyed in the house fire.

The loss was a major blow to my parents. But being homeless with seven children, they didn't have the luxury of wallowing in self-pity.

Immediately, my father looked toward the cinder-block garage that sat on our property and determined this was where we were going to live. Neighbors and family pitched in—my Uncle Joe poured a cement floor and added a 12' X 20' slab for an extra room while neighbors donated furniture. To heat our new home, my father purchased a new kitchen range with a warming oven on top and a hot-water reservoir.

During the construction my brothers bunked at a neighbor's while my parents stayed with Uncle Joe and Aunt Ruby. I had my switchboard job and my apartment in Benton through the week so I was spared the worst of the dirt and sawdust. Within two weeks the doors and windows were hung and the family moved in.

We lived there three years. The remains of the original house were filled in with dirt and grass was sown over the top. I eventually quit my job, sacrificed my apartment in Benton and ended up back home sleeping on the couch once again until I met and married Robert Harvey Jr.

Because my parents didn't carry insurance there was no official investigation and the cause of the fire never was determined. For years I believed it originated from the stove my father installed in the basement, except the fire occurred in the spring—the stove we used for heat wouldn't have been in use at the time. Perhaps my brothers had been playing with matches. It remains a mystery.

By 1947 the oil wells began drying up, forcing my father to look for work again. Brothers Kenneth and Jim Mandrell, who had fled the area for the Quad-Cities, returned bragging about the abundance of good paying jobs building farm machinery.

Taking a month's worth of work in Peoria to fund the trip, my father then pulled my brothers Charles and Bobby out of high school—after coaching them to lie about their ages—and headed to the Quad-Cities where they found jobs at the J. I. Case plant in Bettendorf, Iowa. After their first few paychecks they moved from their sleeping room to an apartment, coming back to Thompsonville for my mother and the rest of the family.

Our three-room "garage" house was sold to the Dunford family. I remained in Thompsonville with my husband, living with his grandmother White in her old farm house.

Young love: Robert and Mable Harvey.
(Photo courtesy of Christopher Gulley.)

10

MR. AND MRS. ROBERT E. HARVEY JR.

Mable Gulley-Harvey

He was wearing an Army uniform and taking a duffle bag out of the trunk the first time I laid eyes on newly discharged Corp. (Tech-Five) Robert E. Harvey Jr. I said nothing to him at the time but made a mental note as I walked past.

Three months later we would be husband and wife.

* * * * * * * * *

My friends from Thompsonville High School had talked me into joining the Baptist church. After Sunday night services we would congregate at the little restaurant where highways 34 and 149 intersected, an area the locals called the "Y".

Some of the girls had boyfriends but I didn't. Robert was pacing back and forth through the restaurant and after the third pass he leaned over our table, looked me in the eye and asked the room, "Who wants to go skating?"

Everyone rushed to their cars for the 15-mile trip to the skating rink in Marion. I was the only girl who said, "I have to ask my father."

Mable Gulley (left) with her church singing group.

"Okay," said Robert, finally speaking directly to me for the first time. "We can drive down to your house before we go."

Three other girls climbed into the car, including Marvella Dunford, who made no secret of her intentions regarding Robert. When I went inside to talk to my father, Marvella slid over next to him, leaving me fuming in the passenger seat all the way to Marion.

After arriving at the skating rink however, Robert ignored Marvella's blatant advances and proceeded to walk me in, buy my ticket and skate with me the whole night. He spent much of our "date" picking me up off the floor because I was a terrible skater. He, on the other hand, was a whirling dervish who could skate backward, turn in circles, and otherwise impress the novices like me who watched in amazement.

On the way home that night Robert dropped me off last but drove away without saying whether he would see me again.

* * * * * * * *

He turned up a week later in Mt. Vernon at my Uncle Johnny Glover's, where I had gone looking for work after leaving the switchboard operator's job in Benton. My

father had told him he could drive me back from Mt. Vernon if he wanted to see me that badly. I still remember him standing in the glare of the headlights with his foot on the front bumper of his car, tying his shoes in the rain.

I couldn't drive. But Robert insisted, claiming he'd seen me behind the wheel of a Model A flying down the road at 20 mph

Miss White's house where Robert and Mable first lived.

with my white-knuckled father in the passenger seat. After I barely missed several cars on the highway, Robert changed his mind and drove us the rest of the way to Thompsonville.

During our three-month courtship we attended church and his parents invited me to Sunday dinners. We caught movies in West Frankfort and went swimming with our friends at Thompsonville Lake.

My father was highly protective of me and my reputation. The lake had no bathhouses for changing so before and after swimming we had to duck behind bushes and hope for privacy. One day we had returned from the lake and rather than risk indecent exposure I had kept my bathing suit on with a towel around my shoulders. My mistake was sitting in the car with Robert and talking because my father stormed out, yanked open the car door and told me to get in the house and get dressed. He meant well but at the time it was humiliating and made me determined to escape his iron-fisted rule.

Robert and I had met in May and by August we knew we wanted to be together. One Sunday Robert's mother saw us sitting on the couch with a road map and asked if we were going somewhere.

"We thought we would drive down to Kentucky and get married," was Robert's

(Photo by Ray Congrove)

casual reply. Kentucky allowed couples to get blood tests, licenses and marry all in the same day.

His mother offered her best poker face and left the room.

We chose a Baptist church in Morganfield. After we produced our paperwork for the minister, a fellow named Stanger, he pointed out that we needed a pair of witnesses for the ceremony. His wife and daughter stood up for us and signed the marriage certificate. The date was Aug. 29, 1947.

We stopped at my parents' house first to share the news. My mother-in-law presented me with a pair of silk pajamas as a wedding gift.

Robert's grandmother, Bess White, had been a widow since March 1947. Her husband Joe had suffered from "hardening of the arteries"—what I suspect they would call Alzheimer's today—and would wander away from their farmhouse, confused and in various stages of undress, until Bess was forced to put him into a nursing facility. She was lonely without him, so when Robert approached her about having us move in, she readily accepted.

Seventy-plus years later, Robert and I still are together.

11

IMMOBILE HOME

Mable Gulley-Harvey

Like many young newlyweds we struggled financially, falling back on the generosity of our relatives. We lived rent-free with my husband's grandmother while running the family service station next door. To shore up our meager earnings we sold ice hauled in from Benton and off-loaded in Thompsonville where we would chip the scored 300-pound slabs into smaller pieces for sale to the public. In addition, each summer we stocked cold watermelon.

After the birth of our first daughter Jill, we began to feel constrained by our living arrangements. But a house of our own seemed out of reach, given our income from the service station.

My in-laws had an out-building next to their home they referred to as "the smokehouse". It was often used to serve Sunday meals after church because it was cooler than the kitchen during the southern Illinois heat waves. However, my mother-in-law was irritated by its proximity to their back

Robert Harvey Jr. with 8-month-old daughter Jill in front of their new "immobile home."

door. My father-in-law owned several lots on Thompsonville's main street. He suggested that we move the smokehouse and combine it with an old wooden garage on one of his properties to make a home.

Bob and his friends jacked up the smokehouse and hammered wooden runners onto each side. They attached chains and, with the help of neighbor Jim Croslin's old Oliver tractor, dragged the smokehouse 3 blocks to the highway where the runners got hung up on the edge of the pavement and wouldn't budge.

Fortunately, another fellow farmer happened by—such was life in a small town where tractors doubled as personal vehicles—and with his extra horsepower they cleared the highway, depositing the smokehouse within four feet of the old wooden garage. We built a hallway to connect the two structures and remodeled the smokehouse into a kitchen while the old garage doubled as our bedroom and living room. There was no indoor plumbing but we did have a sink with a hand-pump for well water and an outhouse out back. For convenience we kept a chamber pot inside.

We lived there with Jill until we moved to the Quad-Cities in 1952. We handed the keys off to my brother-in-law who established his veterinary practice there until he relocated to a bigger building next door.

Miraculously, our former address survived the tornado that roared through Thompsonville on April 27, 1971, damaging my brother-in-law's office (nearly killing my father-in-law who was blown out the side of the building along with a portion of the wall) and leveling Everett and Villa Carlisle's corner market. The damage estimates for the town that day exceeded $500,000.

* * * * * * * * *

The sum of its parts: To the left of the front door is the former "smokehouse", pulled across town by tractor and attached to the previously free-standing garage on the right. This would become the first home of Robert and Mable Harvey.

One of the house's final occupants was Bob's friend Jimmy Elimon who ran the town barber shop which had also been reduced to rubble by the tornado. My father-in-law had allowed him to move his barber shop business into the house, charging him a mere $20 per month rent, a rate that stayed the same for years. After the death of her husband my mother-in-law inherited the place but the original rent agreement remained unchanged. Unfortunately,

even at that low rate Jimmy was lax at paying the rent on time, something I continu-
ally lectured my mother-in-law about.

Jimmy's on-the-job hygiene was equally lax. Unbeknownst to us (and probably
the health department) he would sweep the hair trimmings of his clients into the back
room rather than properly dispose of it. When I visited him at his shop during one of
our infrequent trips back to Thompsonville I
was horrified by the literal carpet of human
hair, a foot high.

"I'm saving it all for my garden," he
joked. "It's protein!"

After her death my mother-in-law, exhibiting a streak of sarcasm from beyond the
grave, willed me the property along with our
hygienically-challenged squatter. I sat down
and addressed twelve envelopes, affixing a
twenty-two cent stamp on each, and presented them to Jimmy in hopes of facilitating payment, along with a belated rent increase. Both
overtures were ignored. In my head, I figured

*Tenant and barber Jimmy Elimon preferred
storing the cut hair of his clients in a back room
rather than properly disposing of it, claiming
the follicles were "protein" for his garden.*

that twenty dollars rent minus two dollars and sixty-four cents for the stamps left us
with seventeen dollars and thirty-six cents. Jimmy soon retired, still ahead of the game.

* * * * * * * * *

The former smokehouse and old garage that was our first home still stands on a
vacant stretch along Route 34, opposite the post office. Time and man has altered its
façade—the exterior is weather beaten and rotting, the vegetation overgrown, the outside painted a ghastly rust-brown by tenants unknown.

I look at the place now through the passing of the years and wonder how we ever
managed.

Brenda Jill Harvey

12

LITTLE FLANNEL NIGHTGOWNS

Mable Gulley-Harvey

I almost died giving birth to my first child.

My husband Bob and I were living with his grandmother White in Thompsonville when I got up from our bed and blood gushed onto the throw rug. Although I'd been present during my mother's deliveries, I was a naive first-timer who assumed heavy bleeding was a normal side-effect of having babies.

I had no idea the trouble I was in.

Bob called his mother Jessie, who contacted Dr. Ahlm, my personal physician. He explained what was happening and urged her to get me to the hospital as fast as possible—although I was in no pain, I was hemorrhaging badly.

Miss White helped me into a robe and folded a large terrycloth towel to put between my legs. Bob ran three blocks to borrow his friend's Plymouth that he thought would be more comfortable for me than our battered 1939 Ford pickup. He helped me into the car as I clutched the towel and we raced the 17 miles to Miner's Hospital in Christopher, stopping in West City to pick up Aunt Ruby.

Duck-walking into the hospital with the bloody towel between my legs, I was escorted to a bed and placed on oxygen. Aunt Ruby sat by me, asking whether I had any pain. Meanwhile, Bob had disappeared. "Oh, you know how men are, he's probably outside smoking," she lied. My situation was so grim he'd gone out frantically soliciting his friends as blood donors.

From left to right: Jill Harvey with Bill Harvey, Robert Harvey Sr., and Lawrence Edward, Arthur Lee and Billy Bob Gulley.

They rushed me into surgery to perform a cesarean. It was crucial they get the baby out to stop me from bleeding to death. After delivering a jaundiced and underweight baby girl, the surgeons turned their attention toward saving me.

The placenta—the organ that provides nourishment and waste elimination for the fetus—had come loose from the uterine wall. The doctors advised Aunt Ruby to contact my parents because it didn't look like I would survive. Later, she told me that when the surgeons came out of the operating room the knees of their coveralls were caked solid with blood.

After I was stabilized and in recovery, my mother and oldest brother Charles drove down from Rock Island to see me. I was lying in bed holding my stomach because I was so sore. Charles kept making me laugh.

I was discharged after one week. The baby, whom we named Brenda Jill, had to remain another two weeks because her birth weight (5 lbs. 8 oz.) had dropped slightly—they wanted her to gain a little more before releasing her.

I wasn't strong enough to nurse, so Jill was bottle-fed two ounces of formula every two hours. She was so small the stores didn't stock any clothing that would fit. Miss White custom-made her dozens of little flannel nightgowns with roses embroidered between the buttons.

A permanent home at last.

13

THE FARM IMPLEMENT CAPITOL OF THE WORLD

Mable Gulley-Harvey

By 1947 Robert Earl Harvey Jr. was a young man in a hurry. Like many who had returned from the war, Bob wanted a home of his own and a means of supporting a family. We already had met and married after a brief courtship of three months and were staying with Miss White in her old farm house. We lacked an income but Bob knew automotive mechanics offered the best employment opportunities.

The David Rankin Trade School was in St. Louis. Bob's G.I. Bill offered $125 per month toward his education, so it was agreed that I would remain in Thompsonville while he made the weekly commute to St. Louis for his automotive classes. He rode with several other young men who lived in nearby Zeigler—the boy that owned the car had lost a leg during the war and the government had given him a specially outfitted vehicle he could operate. He and the others studied refrigeration at the same school. They all lived in sleeping rooms throughout the week and returned home on the weekends.

Upon graduation in 1948, Bob found a job in Galatia, Illinois, fixing cars for a man named Cat Bridwell. He earned $25 per week. We stayed in a one-room apartment but it wasn't our idea of earning a living. There were no jobs for me in those small towns and we struggled to make ends meet.

* * * * * * * * *

My family already had moved north to the Quad-Cities—nicknamed "The Farm Implement Capitol of the World"—and word filtered back how good the money was in the factories. Whether it was because I missed my family or was tired of living hand-to-mouth—or both—I convinced Bob to make the move north where he found an assembly line job at the J.I. Case plant in Bettendorf, Iowa, across the Mississippi River from where we had moved in with my parents. We occupied an upstairs bed-room at 1730 7th Street in Moline, Illinois. I worked for a company that laundered uniforms, operating a machine that sewed on buttons. We owned one car but luckily we worked the same hours so Bob would drop me off and pick me up each day.

Most weekends we would make the 350-mile trek to Thompsonville to see Bob's parents. His father would try and cajole Bob into moving back to Thompsonville, where he was currently operating the service station and feed store while selling ice on the side. His plan involved separating the businesses, moving the feed store up the road to a new building while leaving Bob in charge of the service station and ice house.

Bob resisted his father for months but when J.I. Case laid him off, against our better judgment, we returned to Thompsonville.

During our time in the Quad-Cities, Miss White sold her farm house and built a small four-room home next to the service station. We moved into a back bedroom. After the birth of our first child Jill, Miss White was a great help to me in caring for the baby because I still was recovering from complications of having a caesarean birth. At the end of each day Bob would dump the pocket change earned from selling ice into a jar on our dresser that paid the hospital bill for Jill's birth.

Robert Earl Harvey Sr. could be a kind and generous man but tended to ignore the opinions of others (the new building that housed the feed store was purchased for $10,000 without my mother-in-law's knowledge or consent, to her eternal conster-nation). Bob worked long hours and the personality differences between him and his father became more pronounced. He was a dutiful and respectful son. I heard Bob talk back to his father only once when the elder Harvey criticized him for closing the service station too early, disregarding the hours his son already had logged.

Eventually, we moved out of Miss White's back bedroom to a ramshackle home where we lived over the next few years. Ultimately, we knew a re-location back to the Quad-Cities was in the cards given our financial struggles. When it happened, we gave the service station and ice house back to Bob's father and headed north with few regrets.

* * * * * * * * *

When we arrived in the Quad-Cities, we ended up with my parents again, this time in an area called Harris Addition. There were five small houses on top of a hill across the road from Black Hawk State Historic Site in Rock Island. When one became available we moved in.

There were few amenities. The toilet was outside and water came from a common shared faucet on the hillside. We filled two 10-gallon milk cans and dipped the water out as we needed it. On the plus side, we at least had a refrigerator and a stove that ran on bottled gas. Happily, my parents were neighbors, so my mother and I did the laundry together using her wringer washer and hanging the clothes on a line.

Bob reapplied at his former employer J. I. Case and was hired to work on the factory forklifts. We stayed in Harris Addition until Jill was 4, eventually moving to Moline. There we rented a small 2-room house at 1730 36th Street near Roosevelt Elementary School, where Jill entered kindergarten.

The place was a slight upgrade from our former residence. The attic was big enough for our beds, with running water and a kitchen sink though it lacked a bathroom. We were dependent on Mrs. Pope, the landlady who lived across the driveway, to graciously offer her bathroom so we could bathe

Jill and her doll, Suzy.

(Jill was young enough to wash in the kitchen sink). Bob and I ended up taking many sponge baths for the sake of convenience. We still used an outdoor toilet— illegal inside the city limits—that sat among the trees on the side of a deep ravine.

Jill playing in the yard at the house on 36th Street in Moline, Illinois.

We crossed the landlady's back yard nightly to empty a chamber pot that we kept on the back porch lean-to. Years before we could afford air-conditioning, Bob used his mechanical skills to build a huge window fan for the attic bedroom.

With Jill getting older and too big for bathing in the kitchen sink, we found a nice four-room apartment with a bath at 2033 15th Street, Moline. It was upstairs and we each had our own bedroom. Jill entered the fifth grade at Garfield Elementary school. Although he still was employed at J.I. Case, Bob found a part-time job in Rock Island at

a Texaco station owned by a man named Ted Davies, who would remain his employer for the better part of the next decade.

After a full day at the factory, Bob would come home for dinner and then labor a further three hours each night at the station. When Davies offered him a full-time position Bob accepted, working into the night but enjoying

From left to right: Service station owner Ted Davies, unknown customer, and employee Robert Harvey Jr.

being out of the factory. Whenever Davies and his wife took vacations, Bob was left in charge. We were ordered to take any deposits or receipts and hold them until the couple returned. Sometimes we would have as many as 14 money bags stashed under our bed.

Despite our economic upturns this was the saddest period in my life. Our second child died one day after her birth. I'm sure Bob's heart was broken as well. It seems I cried on his shoulder forever until my doctor advised me to have another baby. A boy named Brad was born one year later. We traveled often to New Salem Park in Springfield, Illinois, to meet Bob's parents and brother who had driven up halfway from Thompsonville to see the new baby.

Our landlady complained about the children running in the hallway. Asking children not to run was like *Brad Harvey rides his tricycle.* asking the wind not to blow. I felt it was time to move once again. Our next-door neighbor liked to work outside on his typewriter while sunbathing, so in passing I learned from him that he was a teacher and would be moving at the end of the school year. Through him we met his landlady and soon we became tenants. The place had only one bedroom but the glassed-in front porch doubled as a spare. It had no heat but we left the double doors open at night and buried ourselves in heavy quilts. Jill and Brad shared the sole bedroom.

* * * * * * * * *

Ted Davies opened a marine dealership called Ted's Boat-A-Rama but Bob was uninterested in doing boat repairs. Instead, Davies offered Bob the Texaco station, selling us the contents outright while Davies' wife taught me the basics of doing the accounting ledgers for the business. We opened a separate business account for the station at the Uptown National Bank in Moline.

The Texaco station became our life for the next four years. We never worked harder and saw fewer rewards financially. We broke even most of the time, although once, when the gasoline truck made its scheduled stop, we had to borrow $2,000 from my mother to pay for the delivery. An acquaintance at our bank learned to hold deposit slips for us while we crossed our fingers that the next day's receipts would cover the amount of the check.

Sometimes the young men we

Robert Harvey Jr. in front of the Texaco station in Rock Island, Illinois.

hired part-time on Sundays to pump gas ended up in the garage working on their own cars and ignoring the customers. We seldom had a real day off because we would spend it monitoring our employees.

Having charge accounts and offering credit was the worst aspect of running the business. It always seemed like the people wearing the nicest clothes and driving the fanciest cars were the biggest deadbeats. I would have to go to their homes to collect the money they owed us and invariably they would be offended by the very notion of having to pay their bills.

The biggest scare we had running the station was when we nearly blew up the place. At closing time we would shut all the lights off outside the station. We would pull our own car up to the pump, insert the nozzle, and go inside to finish up. The pump would shut off automatically when the tank was full. Except this time it didn't.

When we left the inside of the station we saw gasoline gushing down the side of the car onto the driveway and into the street like a torrent of rain. We shut down the pump, grabbed a water hose and flushed the pavement, praying that no passing cars backfired or had drivers flinging lit cigarettes to turn the corner into a hellish conflagration. We kept the whole incident quiet, never knowing how much gasoline we'd hosed into the sewer system.

We got out of the service station business not long after, broke, tired and stressed by the entire experience. Bob collected his tools and decided that his next job would be in one of the many area factories where the unions guaranteed a good wage and decent benefits.

* * * * * * * * *

In the midst of all this I determined we needed a bigger place to live and a little more privacy befitting a growing family. There was a young couple upstairs and we could hear through the paper-thin walls.

For distraction I liked to take Brad and drive around Moline, ending up most days at Grant's, a downtown department store with a luncheon counter. Touring the neighborhoods we came across a two-story house on the corner of 16th Avenue and 11th Street with a "rent" sign in the yard. People were dragging furniture into the garage. As we entered the home, others were steaming off the wallpaper. A woman named Mrs. Hansen had inherited the property from her uncle, a man named Carl Nelson, rumored to have passed away in the upstairs bathroom. The catch was she didn't want to rent to people with children. But after two hours of us hanging around and her seeing how well-behaved Brad was for a 3-year-old, she relented.

At $75 per month, Bob felt we couldn't afford it and balked at the potential heat bills we'd incur if we lived in such a large home. On the plus side, I countered that each of us would have a bedroom and he would have a garage for his tools. Some couples argue and harangue but my logic regarding any major decisions—leaving Thompsonville and coming to the Quad-Cities, for instance—was like a slow dripping faucet, wearing Bob down until I prevailed (although to be fair, I knew Bob would relent if it made me happy). We moved into the house where we would spend the rest of our lives. When it came to basic material items, we were lacking—we owned no bedroom dressers or dining room furniture and I struggled with a wringer washer that shocked me as I fed our wet clothes into it. But even with hanging the wash on a basement clothesline during the winters or ironing all of it at once because we had no dryer, I was in love with this place.

Bob had made a lot of friends while running the Texaco station. One was an amiable little eccentric named Hershel Smith. Good with his hands, Hershel had built his own brick house and was a meticulous woodworker (years later, his skills would extend to sewing a wedding gown for his own daughter!). He was part of the office personnel at International Harvester Company Farmall Works and told Bob to fill out an application, ensuring it was steered into the right inbox. Three weeks later

Bob was part of the line that assembled and adjusted tractor transmissions, holding the position for nearly 23 years until the plant closed and he took retirement at age 62.

When we were firmly ensconced in our new place, we had enough money to pay our bills but nothing left over. Because I was the one that shepherded us into our new home I figured I should be the one to earn some extra money. From an ad I saw in the local newspaper I applied for a job at the Moline Public Library and was hired three days later. Starting pay was only minimum wage at $1.25 an hour but with my check I was able to buy a few things for the house. With Brad one block away at Lincoln Elementary I was able to meet him for lunch each day. Jill was attending nearby John Deere Junior High.

Three years into our lease Mrs. Hansen came to us and explained that she wanted to sell the property. She was tired of the upkeep—roof repairs, painting, and handling the general yard maintenance. Did we wish to buy?

I already loved the house and Bob had established his garage—none of us entertained yet another move. We applied for an FHA (Federal Housing Authority) loan and received enough to meet the asking price of the house: $10,800. Monthly payments started at $72, eventually rising to $150 on 30 years at 5.25 percent interest.

Only briefly did we consider uprooting and heading back to Thompsonville. Anticipating our retirement we bought some property on the east side of town and spent the summer building a massive garage, with a bathroom and enough attic space for living quarters. My Uncle Joe laid the cement with his oldest son Billy Gene and my brothers, Bobby and Lawrence Edward, helped with the framing. Brad, now in his early teens, tamped down sand for the foundation, stapled insulation, and with Bob, shingled the roof.

Construction of a house was supposed to be next. But in the end we realized that we had been gone from the area for so long that it just didn't feel like home any more. We sold the place and never spoke of moving again. After a lifetime of upheavals and countless residences we realized that in the Quad-Cities we already had found the home we were looking for.

Don Gulley (left) with his band, The Westernaires. (Photo courtesy of Sue Gulley-Winters)

COUNTRY SON

Brad Harvey

"What do ya know, Bradley Joe?"

I'm 14 and my Uncle Don is in our kitchen laying out a guitar case across the table, popping open the lid and revealing his latest purchase: a blonde Epiphone acoustic. He pulls the instrument out and hands it to me, asking me to check it out. I've only been a guitarist for a few months but I'm flattered that my opinion matters.

I go through my limited repertoire of chords, taking note of the instrument's bold ringing tones and easy action. I'm still stuck with my beginner guitar, a nylon-stringed Yamaha sporting a neck the width of a railroad tie (though I would eventually master "The Who Live At Leeds" in its entirety on this accursed tree trunk, I didn't yet grasp my parents' logic e.g. starting your kid on something cheap until his level of commitment can be gauged). But I'm definitely elated at getting my hands on a superior instrument.

"You want to play it a while?" he asks, leaving it in my care just long enough to suffer withdrawal pangs when he eventually reclaims it.

It's the last I see of that particular guitar. Don shows up weeks later with a new one nowhere near the quality of the Epiphone. When I ask about it, I'm fobbed off with the excuse, "Aw, I didn't like it."

I learn later that my Aunt Sally, in a fit of rage at her husband, had taken a hacksaw to its neck.

Don and Sally Gulley

"I prefer to think they were passionate," my cousin said to me about the sometimes-tempestuous relationship between her parents. My own theory is that, like most long-term couples, they knew how to bring the craziness out in each other.

* * * * * * * * *

Born Donald Eugene Gulley Nov. 17, 1933, Don was number four in a family of seven children, all of them boys except for my mother.

Don's older brother Bobby once told me that of all the Gulley siblings, Don was the one he feared the most because of a murderous temper inherited from their father. "Don didn't know when to quit," my mother said about her younger brother's propensity for bucking authority and brawling with anyone who might try controlling him. Younger brother Lawrence Edward, himself a participant in numerous physical confrontations with his brother, recalled a teenage Don and his friends fleeing from the police, driving a car at high speed across their parents' front lawn with the law in hot pursuit.

My grandfather, already stressed from the demands of raising a large family plus fearing jail-time for his wayward boy, no doubt pressured his son into taking some responsibility over his life. Ludicrously, the boy who hated being told what to do—and who couldn't swim—joined the Navy in 1952.

Not even the military could rein Don in for very long. Being AWOL—Absent Without Leave—my grandparents would drive him back to the Great Lakes Training Center in Chicago where he would flee, oftentimes beating them back to the family home in Rock Island County. He hid out for a time in nearby Erie, running with a crowd that included a man later charged with murdering a girlfriend. Eventually, Don was caught, sentenced and transported from Great Lakes cross-country to Portsmouth Naval Prison, a bleak structure of reinforced concrete across the river from Portsmouth, New Hampshire on Seavey Island (modeled after Alcatraz).

Don Gulley

Lawrence Edward, in the Air Force and stationed nearby at Grenier Air Force Base in Manchester, New Hampshire (now the Manchester-Boston Regional Airport), recalls seeing Don on a prison van "looking scared for his life." He was the only family member to visit during Don's incarceration.

After serving his sentence, Don was dishonorably discharged from the military in 1954 and came back to the Quad-Cities, no doubt changed by the experience and anxious to pull his life together. He married Sally Ellen Harker Aug. 28, 1954 and the union produced three children: Darci Jean, born 1955; Susan Dawn, born 1959; and Gregory Donald, born 1967. He secured a permanent position with John Deere Harvester in East Moline and his life seemed set.

Don and Sally Gulley (Photo courtesy of Sue Gulley-Winters.)

* * * * * * * * *

It was Don's father-in-law who introduced him to the guitar at the age of 22, showing him the basic chords to "You Are My Sunshine", which the budding musician proceeded to play endlessly, to the irritation of the household.

Blessed with a booming baritone and an outgoing personality, Don was always the loudest voice in the room and a natural storyteller who loved Johnny Cash, Hank Williams, and Jim Croce. At funerals, he could reduce mourners to tears—and on occasion himself—when asked to eulogize the departed with his rendition

of "Green, Green Grass of Home." In demand as a vocalist, he fronted country acts The Westernaires, R.C.'s Nightshift and later—asserting his drawing power at the Moose and V.F.W. dances that were their bread and butter—Don Gulley and the Country Sons.

The lineups fluctuated depending on player availability (and equally, who fought with whom). The band's sound was raw and no frills, held aloft

Don Gulley mastering the chords to "You Are My Sunshine." (Photo courtesy of Sue Gulley-Winters)

some nights by nothing more than Don's powerhouse vocals. They would strip songs down to the bare bones rather than figure out all the chords, something I learned when I took the stage with the band for a bash at Roy Orbison's "Pretty Woman". While they pounded in unison through their gutted version I floundered like an amateur, play-ing it just like the record.

The volunteer gigs Don and I did for the local adult daycare center remain my favorite musical memory. Armed with acoustic guitars, I would back Don while he

wailed "Bad, Bad Leroy Brown", "Rhinestone Cowboy" and "The Fireman" to a captive au-dience of stroke patients and people suffer-ing dementia.

The music would animate them in strange ways. We were approached by a man with Alzheimer's and asked if we knew "When the Saints Go Marching In." Don and I looked at each other as the man produced a harmonica from his shirt pocket and proceed-ed to play. We backed him the best we could, marveling at his ability on the instrument.

Brad Harvey and Don Gulley performing.

When we finished, the man turned to us and asked if we knew "When the Saints Go Marching In" before launching into it a second, third and fourth time until his caregiver rescued us from a fifth go-round.

* * * * * * * * *

Tired of lugging amplifiers in and out of V.F.W. halls and the like, Don declared his performing days were behind him and broke up his band. He stayed busy after retirement from John Deere Harvester, acquiring a four-unit apartment house next door to his Davenport home and becoming a landlord. He reveled in being a grand-parent.

My Aunt Sally—as colorful a character as her husband—succumbed to cancer in 2008.

Don, a smoker much of his life, died 10 months later in 2009 from an enlarged heart. At his funeral there was no one to sing "Green, Green Grass of Home" but an unknown mourner saw fit to place a guitar pick on his casket.

Lawrence Edward Gulley

15

LAST MAN STANDING

Mable Gulley-Harvey

Lawrence Edward was the brother we all feared would meet a bad end because of alcoholism. Two of our uncles suffered from the disease—one of them, Rex Aaron, was found dead leaning against the back fence of his vegetable garden, his bottle beside him. A hard drinker much of his life, we figured he had paused to take a swig and collapsed on the spot.

I was 8 on May 11, 1936, when Lawrence Edward was born. I was mad at my mother for giving birth to another boy. I already had three brothers and longed for a little sister.

As with the rest of us, Lawrence Edward had been birthed at home with Dr. Moore and my Aunt Ruby attending. My mother lay in a double bed in the living room with Dr. Moore administering a cloth doused with chloroform over her mouth when the labor pains became severe.

Once my mother had pushed the baby out, Dr. Moore handed him off to Aunt Ruby. With the newborn cradled in her arms she walked into the kitchen and took a seat in front of the cook stove, its door open. In the warmth of the fire,

Rex Aaron in 1967.

she washed the after-birth from his body and wrapped him in a well-worn blanket. She placed him next to my mother who lay exhausted in the darkened room. He was named Lawrence Edward for his father and the birth recorded at the Franklin County Courthouse in Benton, Illinois.

* * * * * * * * *

By the time my father had moved us into a small farm north of Galatia, Illinois, Lawrence Edward was no longer the baby. We had another brother named Arthur Lee who was nearing his third birthday and my mother was already carrying her seventh (and final) child that I got to name Billy Bob and who would weigh in at more than 13 pounds at birth.

With an eye toward selling milk to the local dairy my father had purchased six milk cows and two work horses for tilling the fields. The older boys would milk while my father would struggle with a plow that turned over only one row of dirt at a time. He would clutch it with both hands and throw the reins of the horse over his shoulders while my brothers ran behind so they could see the snakes slither out of the plowed dirt. All of us attended school a mile away in a one-room building at an intersection which also had a grocery store. The area, called Cornerville, was barely big enough to be worthy of a name.

Finances and calamity (job losses and a house fire) determined our next three moves. But by this time my father had heard about the great-paying jobs up north from a couple of brothers named Mandrell. My husband recalled what really impressed people was the brand-new car one of the Mandrells drove, bought with northern factory wages.

Once my father, along with Charles and Bobby, had gotten jobs and established residency in the Quad-Cities, they returned for my mother plus Don, Lawrence Edward, Arthur Lee and Billy Bob, all of them excited about moving to a new place. With help from the boys, my father removed the back seat of the car so they could all stretch their legs into the trunk and sleep in intervals over the 350-mile trip.

Arriving at the new place—a chicken house in Castle Junction hastily converted into living quarters—the boys set about the neighborhood, checking out the sights and making friends. In the fall, they were all enrolled at the nearby one-room schoolhouse.

My parents were not ones to attend teacher conferences or PTA meetings. They simply pointed their children in the direction of the school and trusted them to make their way forth. Only when the report cards were issued did they show interest in the education of their offspring.

After a stint in Castle Junction the family relocated to Rock Island's Harris Addition opposite Black Hawk State Historic Site, a 208 acre forest and nature preserve. Lawrence Edward and Arthur Lee were slated to attend Franklin Junior High on Ninth Street. Unbeknownst to their parents, the two brothers had spent their first weeks of school playing hooky in the woods. When they returned early one afternoon because of a torrential rain, my mother eyed her two boys with suspicion. A call to the school confirmed that no students had ever registered—or attended— under the name "Gulley."

That night the boys sat frozen with fear at the dinner table. Our father had a violent temper and the two knew there was no way they were going to escape punishment. We used to say that with having so many boys under his roof, our father "had to have his bluff in" to maintain order. His methods might entail using an open hand or closed fist, a belt, or "whipping up a batch of hickory tea" where the child would be sent into the woods to retrieve a switch with which to be beaten about the legs. Occasionally what he would term discipline would cross the line into abuse and our mother would intercede.

Adhering to his father's credo that he must do something whether attending school or finding a job, Lawrence Edward opted for employment. He knew a young man named Bud Gates whose parents had removed him from school and gotten him night work greasing baking pans at the Coin Baking Co. in Rock Island (Greek in origin, the well-to-do Coin family would remain in Lawrence Edward's life even through his worst years of alcoholism).

Despite the age difference between the two—Bud, 14, Lawrence Edward, 16— they became best friends. Bud's father got Lawrence Edward a job taking hot loaves out of the ovens. Bud lived on the same street as the Joseph McGuire family and Lawrence Edward began dating their daughter Betty. They would eventually become engaged.

When Lawrence Edward was 17 he and Bud decided to join the Air Force. Since Bud had limited education Lawrence Edward helped him fill out the proper forms. With two other young men they boarded a bus to Chicago for the recruiting station where the duo made it through testing and were accepted into the military, pending permission from their parents as they were both under the age of 18.

Betty McGuire-Gulley

Assured Betty would be waiting upon his return, Lawrence Edward left his future bride with her parents and joined Bud for basic training at Sampson Air Force Base in Geneva, New York, with advanced training at Grenier Air Force Base in Manchester, New Hampshire (Lawrence Edward would visit our brother Don during his incarceration for being AWOL at nearby Portsmouth Naval Prison). The two friends were separated when orders sent Bud to Lackland Air Base in Texas and on to Korea as a unit cook while Lawrence Edward was stationed at Hickam Field in Hawaii.

* * * * * * * * *

A few months into his hitch Lawrence Edward received a disturbing letter from Betty back in Rock Island. She informed him that if he didn't come back and marry her by a specific deadline, she would accept the proposal from another boy she had been seeing during Lawrence Edward's tour of duty. It was emotional blackmail but Lawrence Edward borrowed money from The Salvation Army for a return ticket and rushed back to Rock Island under a one-month moral leave from the Air Force. The two married in the Catholic church with a reception in the McGuire family's backyard.

Lawrence Edward returned to Hawaii, followed by Betty a month later. They lived off-base but it was hard on the couple financially. Once Betty became pregnant with their first child Lawrence Edward sought a hardship discharge. He had been in the Air Force for two years. The newlyweds booked passage on the Answorth, docking in California and making their way back to Rock Island, settling in an apartment near Augustana College. Lawrence Edward resumed his duties at the Coin Bakery and within a few short years rose to foreman. Later, he was elected the company's union agent and given an office in downtown Davenport, Iowa.

Lawrence Edward Gulley (left) relaxing with little brother Billy Bob. (Photo courtesy of Sue Gulley-Winters.)

With a loan of $500 from his mother-in-law, he and Betty purchased their first home in nearby Coal Valley, Illinois. In rapid succession the couple had four more children. From the outside it appeared as though they were simply another young family with all the typical struggles wrought by immaturity and inexperience.

Between his responsibilities at work and his duties as husband and father, the pressures began to eat away at Lawrence Edward's resolve. He began to drink and on occasion his secretary would cover for him during his increasing absences. Passed out in his car, he would often wake up in an area of town he wouldn't recognize, marveling at the fact he hadn't run over anyone.

Betty, too, found herself overwhelmed as the mother of five children (Trudy, Becky, Julie, Marshall, and John, in order of birth) tethered to a man whose behavior was becoming erratic and unpredictable. Her own petulance—she wasn't above the same emotional blackmail used earlier to manipulate an already bad situation—precluded her from accepting equal blame for the breakdown of the marriage. If the world wanted to believe she was the innocent victim of an abusive alcoholic, she used it as justification for her own indiscretions.

The couple sold their Coal Valley home and moved to Moline, in theory so that Lawrence Edward could have an easier commute to his Davenport job. But the two continued to take out their mutual frustrations on each other. When Lawrence Edward would come home drunk—triggered by a round of verbal abuse from Betty—she often would lock him out of the house. During one altercation Betty, along with her mother, threw all of his belongings onto the front lawn. Betty's brother, an officer with the Rock Island Police Department, would threaten Lawrence Edward with arrest and worse, based on nothing but Betty's hearsay.

Lawrence Edward would show up at our address, full of rage and vague threats against his wife. He would pass out on our couch and once sober would sit at our kitchen table for hours rehashing the events that derailed his life.

His employers understood—there's evidence they urged him to seek treatment for his alcoholism—but they also had a business to run. He was either fired or forced to resign. Betty filed for divorce but her refusal to sign off on crucial legal documents stalled months of negotiations—petulance to the fore—and so frustrated Lawrence Edward that he, in his own words, "kicked over the table and left town." He fled briefly to Denver, Colorado, where his brother Arthur Lee was living and managed three weeks working at a Safeway bakery, sending money back to us so we could buy groceries for his children.

He did make some genuine efforts toward sobriety. I drove him to a treatment center in Knoxville, Iowa, for 30 days of rehabilitation. The East Moline Mental Health Center also offered an alcohol-treatment program. There was no segregation between the mental-health patients and those receiving help for addiction. Lawrence Edward characterized his time there as something resembling "One Flew over the Cuckoo's Nest." He would try to organize the residents into softball teams, although many lacked the wherewithal to duck when balls were thrown full force at their heads. A cook was relieved of kitchen duties when authorities discovered the man performing indecent acts with the food. "You talk about a load of nuts," Lawrence Edward would say of this period. "I was drunk, not crazy!"

* * * * * * * *

Good-looking and blessed with an easy-going charm, Lawrence Edward never had problems attracting women. Many thought that with a little love and understanding they could rehabilitate him. During his stay at the East Moline Mental Health Center, he became friendly with an attractive young divorcee with two small boys. They moved to Missouri together where Lawrence Edward attended school and eventually earned an associate's degree in technology. While there he learned his divorce from Betty had been finalized, which triggered another bout of drinking. The woman summoned her father to take her and her boys back to the Quad-Cities.

Lawrence Edward Gulley on a rare trip home to Thompsonville.

* * * * * * * *

In Davenport, Lawrence Edward staggered down the boulevard with a bottle and passed out in a parking lot, where he was discovered by a woman named Sandy who was part of a motel cleaning service. A single mother with eight children, she moved him into her home and the two soon married. When the inevitable split happened, Lawrence Edward was back on the streets for another round of drunken degradation.

He found shelter along the Mississippi River in an area under the bridges nicknamed "the jungle" by the homeless people who resided there. He survived a stabbing at a downtown Davenport bar owing to the thickness of his borrowed fur coat—only when he returned to his sleeping room and lay down did he realize the wetness oozing down his side was blood. During another altercation on the streets an unknown assailant smashed him in the head with a brick.

All of us tried to help. I believe our mother gave him money. Many offered him a place to sleep. Billy Bob employed him for a short time until Lawrence Edward showed up drunk and the episode ended in a fight. I felt sorry for him and made sure he had somewhere to go during holidays like Thanksgiving and Christmas. But collectively all of us were burned out. I grew to understand that alcoholism was a disease. Some in the family thought it was a conscious choice.

* * * * * * * * *

There were periods where Lawrence Edward would vanish from our lives. We had no idea if he were alive or dead. He was enterprising and street smart enough to know every food pantry, rescue mission and relief agency, plus his veteran's status guaranteed him medical treatment at the VA hospitals. But he was my brother and I couldn't stop worrying about him.

His younger brother Arthur Lee would remain Lawrence Edward's best friend. He had always welcomed him into his home in Tulsa, Oklahoma, but even brotherly love had its limits. One night while drunk Lawrence Edward aimed a revolver at Arthur Lee and pulled the trigger. The shot missed but in the aftermath Lawrence Edward was shown the door. He was on the streets again, spending Christmas at a homeless encampment called Wine Ridge where, in tribute to the holiday season, the winos had erected a Christmas tree out of empty liquor bottles. It was two days before one of them noticed an acquaintance presumed sleeping in the camp actually was dead.

Lawrence Edward made his way to Kansas. In the course of stealing food from a warehouse he barely escaped arrest. While drinking with students from a nearby technical college, they sent him to pawn a stolen boom box. The clerk ran a quick check on the serial numbers and summoned the police. Considered a homeless drifter, the judge sentenced Lawrence Edward to 10 years in Leavenworth Prison for possession of stolen property. While out on work release he walked down to the Greyhound station and boarded a bus for Springfield, Missouri, where he was picked up and extradited back to Kansas to serve out his remaining sentence.

An attorney representing another inmate overheard Lawrence Edward's story and got him a reduced sentence and early release.

Arriving in Nashville, Tennessee, he took shelter under the bridges spanning the Cumberland River just off the downtown. The Capitol Hotel offered him a position on the maintenance crew—one of his running buddies was a nephew of country singer Webb Pierce—which allowed him a chance to shower daily and clean his clothes before returning to the bridge each night. With the help of The Salvation Army he got himself a small apartment and in short order had a girlfriend and access to a car, only to lose all of it after another relapse.

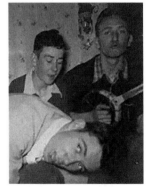

More and more Gulley brothers. Donald Eugene (foreground), Lawrence Edward and Bobby. (Photo courtesy of Sue Gulley-Winters.)

Lawrence Edward ponders his hard-fought life.

On the move again, he landed in Indianapolis, Indiana, and found food and shelter through a church. He fell into yet another relationship but it was always hard to tell how vested Lawrence Edward was in any woman who tried and failed to save him from himself.

* * * * * * * *

When the lure of family became too strong to resist—or maybe feeling the chill of the world closing in—he would always return to the Quad-Cities. One day while standing outside the post office in downtown Rock Island, he met a woman named Mary who lived in nearby Spencer Towers, a low-income senior citizens high-rise. The two struck up a friendship—her former husband had been an alcoholic—and became a couple, eventually settling in Milan, Illinois.

Lawrence Edward was 60 and by his own estimate had been a hardcore drinker for 25 years. As he walked out onto the back porch of their rented house, his leg broke through the rotting planks and he fell into the fissure up to his thigh. Mary called an ambulance and in due course he was transferred to the VA Hospital in Iowa City, Iowa. The surgeons pumped 18 liters of fluid from his booze-bloated belly. A doctor viewing Lawrence Edward as another doomed alcohol casualty coolly pronounced he had two choices: hope for a liver transplant or be dead from drinking in three months.

Amazingly, Lawrence Edward stopped drinking.

Over the next few years he would find steady employment as a maintenance worker at John Deere Commons in Moline. Through the Veterans Administration he secured a loan and purchased a modest home in Rock Island. He rekindled relationships thought lost during the wilderness of his alcoholism.

Ironically, the man many in the family thought likely to die years be-

One of the last photos of the surviving Gulley siblings together, taken in 2008. From left to right: Donald Eugene, Mable Gulley-Harvey, Arthur Lee, Lawrence Edward, and Billy Bob.

fore his time outlived three of his brothers. His eldest son Lawrence Marshall Gulley, after serving 20 years in the United States Navy as a military policeman, began to exhibit the same signs of alcoholism as his father. Diagnosed with cancer, he died in his sleep from internal bleeding in June of 2005. Lawrence Edward's first wife and mother of his children, Betty, passed away in July of 2016. After a short stint in a nursing facility, Mary died in 2017.

Lawrence Edward's knees bother him these days—there have been occasions where the fire department has had to rescue him after falls in the home left him incapacitated. Proud of his sobriety, he brags of "putting nothing stronger than Tylenol in this body!"

If all goes according to plan he fully expects to be around on May 11, 2036, when he turns 100.

(With additional material by Brad Harvey.)

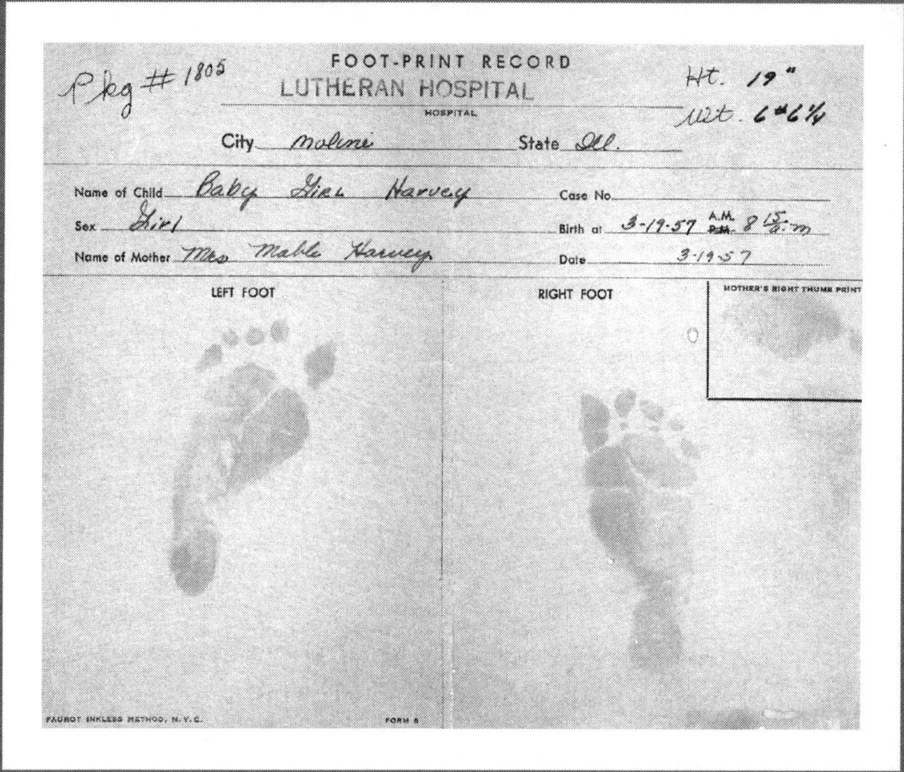

FOOT-PRINT RECORD
LUTHERAN HOSPITAL
HOSPITAL

Pkg # 1805

Ht. 19"

Wt. 6# 6¾

City Moline   State Ill.

Name of Child Baby Girl Harvey   Case No.

Sex Girl   Birth at 3-19-57 A.M. 8 ½ m
                                                          P.M.

Name of Mother Mrs. Mable Harvey   Date 3-19-57

LEFT FOOT	RIGHT FOOT	MOTHER'S RIGHT THUMB PRINT

FAUROT INKLESS METHOD, N.Y.C.   FORM 8

The footprint record of Lu Ann Harvey. She would not survive the next 24 hours.

LU ANN

Mable Gulley-Harvey

Dr. Nash walked into my room at Lutheran Hospital, glanced over at my husband Bob and asked, "Did you tell her?"

He shook his head. Dr. Nash looked at me, took my hand, and after a moment, just said it.

"Your baby girl died last night."

I started to cry. Lu Ann dead? This can't be true, I thought. They'd just shown her to me the day she was born, her head cradled in the nurse's arms, black hair just like her father's. Was she alive then?

* * * * * * * * *

Bob and my father made funeral arrangements for Lu Ann while I lay grief-stricken in the hospital, my stomach stitched and bandaged from the cesarean. Though I would learn through Dr. Nash the cause of Lu Ann's death—her lungs were not fully developed—because of my fragile emotional state I was not allowed to read the autopsy report.

After being discharged, I went home to all the baby things we had purchased over the months. I cried every time anyone looked at me or mentioned the baby. Thinking I'd bear no more children, I gave all of Lu Ann's things to my two pregnant sisters-in-law.

The director of Wheelan Funeral Home didn't like the idea of my husband loading Lu Ann's casket into our 1947 Lincoln and driving the 350 miles to southern Illinois for burial, suggesting it be "hidden" in the trunk so it couldn't be seen. My father swore at the man and the small casket was placed in the back seat of the car.

My father-in-law purchased three lots in the Masonic and Odd Fellows cemetery in Benton, Illinois and gave us the deed, dated March 22, 1957. Lu Ann was buried in Lot 45, section Q near my husband's grandparents, Joe and Bessie White. We didn't have the money for a headstone so my uncle Joe, a cement finisher by trade, made a small, square monument and placed Lu Ann's name on it from letters he'd purchased from the local hardware store. We never did replace it.

Days later my husband was back at work, our daughter Jill was in Garfield Elementary, and I was going through the motions of keeping house. I felt lost.

* * * * * * * * *

I took a job at Lutheran Hospital where Lu Ann had died, typing reports for tests ordered by the doctors and delivering them to the nurses' stations on each floor. Before leaving for the day I would compile a list of surgeries being performed the next morning because this was how they determined if there was enough blood on hand for transfusions. I also delivered pints of blood to the nurses in the operating rooms.

I applied for the job thinking it was a way of getting someone to show me Lu Ann's autopsy report. I would mention it in passing to the people working in the laboratory but they would dissuade me. "Now, you don't want to see that." I stayed with the job for eight months and never saw the report.

I was still sad. I often cried myself to sleep. Dr. Nash was more than my personal physician—our daughters were classmates and friends. She understood. "The only

Mable Gulley-Harvey with new baby boy, Brad Harvey.

way you will ever get over losing this baby is to have another," she said. I was 29.

One year and eight months after Lu Ann's death I had a healthy baby boy. We named him Bradley Joe, after World War II General Omar Bradley and my uncle Joe, who had made Lu Ann's headstone.

After all these years I still wonder if Lu Ann was more disabled than I was told and if the doctors in their mercy just let her slip away. In my mind's eye I still see that head of black hair.

Lawrence Gulley celebrates another year of living.

THE COST OF LIVING

Mable Gulley-Harvey

At the time of his death my father was employed as a crane operator at the Roy E. Roth Co., 2420 4th Ave., Rock Island, a position he'd held for seven years. The company was a steel supplier to all the major farm-machinery manufacturers in the area including Deere & Co., Farmall and J. I. Case.

On Aug. 11 shortly after 1 p.m. my father was on the job attempting to maneuver a flatbed cart loaded with 5,000 pounds of sheet steel used to fabricate gas tanks onto a hydraulic lift. As it rose in the air the load shifted forward, violently propelling the cart backwards toward my father who was struck in the chest by the cart handle. The force of the blow knocked him to the ground.

By the time the police arrived at 1:30, he already had succumbed to his injuries. He was pronounced dead on arrival at Rock Island's St. Anthony's Hospital at 1:45. Coroner Leslie H. Banning declared death was caused by "chest injuries and that extensive internal hemorrhage resulted."

The news of my father's accident reached my husband first. The family scrambled to contact my mother who lived in Matherville, a small town 30

Josie and Lawrence Gulley, 1949.

minutes south of the Quad-Cities. She and my father had no telephone and we feared she would hear the news over the radio before she was prepared emotionally.

Services were held at Hodgson Funeral Home, with burial Aug. 14 at the Memorial Park Cemetery, Rock Island. My brothers were pall bearers.

I convinced my mother to move in with us until she could adjust to living without my father. Lawyers representing the Roy E. Roth Co. came by 13 days after the funeral and took a handwritten statement from her:

STATEMENT FOR THE ATTORNEYS OF ROY E. ROTH COMPANY

Report of Josie E. Gulley, taken in Moline, Illinois on 8-27-59

My name is Josie Evelyn Gulley and I live in Matherville, Illinois. I have no phone.

I am 53 years old and my maiden name was Aaron. Lawrence and myself {sic} were married on 2-4-28 by George B. Moore, J.P. (Justice of the Peace) at Benton, Ill.

My home address before my marriage was Thompsonville and Lawrence {sic} was Ina, Ill.

We had seven children from our marriage.

Mable Jane, 31 years old, Charles Joseph, 29 years old, Robert Earl, 27 years old, Donald Eugene, 26 years old, Lawrence Edward, 23 years old, Albert {Arthur} Lee, 21 years old, Billy Bob, 17 years old, on October 30, 1941, ages of children (when father was killed), all born in Benton, Illinois.

Since our marriage Lawrence and I have lived together and he was my sole support. Neither myself {sic} or Lawrence were ever married before. Lawrence had been employed by Roy Roth for about 7 {sic} years.

I have read the above statement and it is all true and correct.

Josie E. Gulley

My brothers Charles and Bobby were adamant that my mother sue my father's employer for wrongful death. "That building is dangerous," stressed Bobby. "There's loose electrical wires hanging from the ceiling and water puddles on the floor!"

But my mother, still reeling from the shock of losing her husband, hadn't the temperament for a long, drawn-out legal battle. "Mr. Roth and Lawrence were good friends," she said. "I won't sue one of Lawrence's friends." For all of life's unfairness, my mother still took people at face value.

She signed a release and the attorneys for Roy E. Roth presented her with a settlement check for $12,000. It covered my father's funeral expenses plus the cost of two plots and a bronze headstone in Rock Island's Memorial Park Cemetery. After paying off the mortgage on her Matherville home she was left with $500.

She and my father had never owned a bank account or written a check. They

Josie and Lawrence Gulley with one of their many grandchildren.

paid their bills with cash and money orders. I talked her into opening a checking account and depositing the remainder of the settlement money but my mother was steadfast in her refusal to write checks. Several months later we closed the inactive

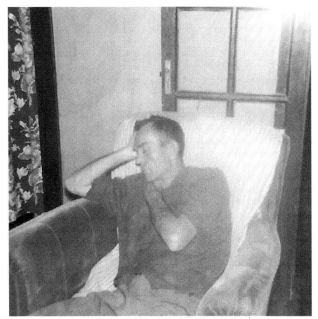

account and put the cash in her hands.

The Roy E. Roth Co. eventually relocated to Milan, Illinois, and is still in business today. The building where my father died was torn down years ago and the site remains empty.

He was 53 when he was killed. The irony of my father's death being reduced to a dollar amount on a piece of legalese was not lost on me.

Arthur Lee Gulley with first wife Fran and two of their children, Timmy and Carrie.

ARTFUL DODGER

Brad Harvey

My Uncle Art was the first adult male I ever knew to use hairspray. Heavily lacquered, his swept-back pompadour rivaled late actor Jack Lord's for aerodynamic ballast. He was dead chuffed when a woman at the airport once mistook him for Glen Campbell, discounting the fact he looked absolutely nothing like the Rhinestone Cowboy.

It would follow that a man with one eye on the mirror would also be an inveterate womanizer. Tales abound of his juggling girlfriends from Rock Island to Tulsa, never mind if a live-in already was sharing his bed. He fathered an out-of-wedlock child in Denver.

Of course such scenarios created endless drama, but Art was blessed with a Teflon heart. No problem, favor, or obligation was too big to be ignored or dismissed with an indifferent shrug. His conscience remained as impervious as his lacquered hair.

* * * * * * * * *

Arthur Lee Gulley was born March 20, 1938, but my grandparents couldn't be bothered to correct the wrong name on his birth certificate, recorded by the attending physician as "Albert." Henceforth, he would be "Art" to the family while the world called him "Albert" or "Al." With five children already under their roof, my grandparents were clearly blasé about the whole matter.

Art's life would have been an asterisk on the Gulley family tree had he not survived being kicked between the eyes by a colt at age three. He grew closest to his older brother Lawrence Edward, and the two would remain a slippery presence within the halls of the public school system. When Lawrence Edward opted for a stint in the United States Air Force, Art followed suit. The normally taciturn recruit fell into an argument with the company paymaster that ended in a fist fight, resulting in a Bad Conduct Discharge.

While lolling back in the Gulley family home in Harris Addition, Rock Island, he met a pretty 15-year-old named Francis "Fran" Evelyn Estell. Anxious to escape a fractious home life, she eloped with Art in October of 1956. He borrowed a vehicle from younger brother Billy Bob and the couple drove to Tulsa, Oklahoma, where Art found work as a baker with Wonder Bread. When Billy Bob retrieved his car there was a diaper lashed to the chassis holding a damaged door in place. Art denied all responsibility and Billy Bob was left footing the bill for repairs.

The union produced three children: Timothy, Carrie, and Cassandra, respectively. Art and Fran divorced in 1968 and he would stay closest with the children of his first marriage. Fran wed WAKY radio personality John Randolph Aspenleiter a.k.a. "Johnny Randolph" and would enter the field herself as both a broadcaster and producer.

Looking for a fresh start, Art transferred to Denver, where he met an attractive brunette named Judy who became pregnant with a daughter they christened Tina. He brought them to the Quad-Cities for a visit and I remember Judy admiring the four   *Arthur Lee with daughter Tina.* smiling band members on the cover of my "Fresh Raspberries" record album. She and Art would soon split and none of us ever saw the little girl again. It's not known whether Art maintained contact with Judy or their daughter, although we suspected they were the principle reason he fled Denver.

* * * * * * * * *

Single and back in the Quad-Cities, he hooked up with his brother Lawrence Edward, who by this time was a textbook alcoholic. Lawrence Edward was accepting of his younger sibling's moral lapses while Art possessed the laissez faire temperament to deal with his older brother's booze-addled mood swings. The two tried their hand at various money-making schemes and settled on becoming painters and roofers. They dubbed their company Gulley Brothers Roofing and promptly ordered checks with my parents' address, without my parents' knowledge or consent.

Thinking they could rush through jobs wielding rented spray-painting equipment—less laborious than applying paint by hand with a brush—disgruntled customers quickly noted the difference in quality between paint manually applied versus the spray gun blotchiness favored by the hit-and-run Gulley brothers. When another client pointed out a bow in the roof the two had shingled and withheld payment, Art slipped into the attic with a carjack and raised the sinking beam to its required height, fleeing before the unsuspecting customer discovered the bogus fix.

Arthur Lee with daughter Stacey.

The partnership floundered when Art, thinking Lawrence Edward too soused to notice, began dipping into the business account and stiffing his brother. Angry and hurt by Art's flagrant dishonesty, Lawrence Edward still was prepared to suck it up and stand by his little brother, no matter how ill-fated the circumstances.

Art bluffed his way into a job driving an 18-wheeler from a warehouse in the Quad-Cities to several delivery stops throughout Chicago and Iowa. Ever loyal, Lawrence Edward arrived to help his inexperienced brother hook up the trailer and then followed him by car several miles until assured Art was safely on his way.

What would otherwise have been an impressive journey by a novice trucker was marred when Art, crossing over a converted railroad bridge, caught the rear of the trailer on the retaining wall sending the 18-wheeler ping-ponging against the opposite sides of the bridge causing a portion of the roadway to drop into the water below. The tractor-trailer was totaled but miraculously Art survived the incident with a few tell-tale glass slivers in his neck. Over the next few weeks he rode the couches of his relatives whose sympathy over the accident was soon superseded by quiet rage at The Man Who Came to Dinner.

He was married briefly to a woman named Norma who was the widow of a police officer and single parent to two teenagers. She gave birth to Art's fifth child, a girl they named Stacey. While Art babysat, Norma went to the courthouse and filed divorce papers. As with his previous relationship, after Art left the Quad-Cities it's unclear whether he remained in touch with the mother or their little girl.

Art returned to the familiarity of Tulsa where he retired from Wonder Bread after nearly three decades while also serving a term as a business manager and president of his local bakers union. He cultivated an interest in Gulley family history, spending hours combing through online court documents and cemetery records.

At his daughter's behest, he relocated to Jacksonville, Florida, to be nearer his grandchildren, signing on as a security guard for the city. He met and married an office worker and part-time piano teacher named Yvonne who brought him into her church family. By most accounts he was a well-liked mainstay of the community.

He journeyed to the Quad-Cities one last time to attend the funeral of his older brother Don. Weeks later, Art suffered a massive stroke. His family held hope he would recover but Art slipped into a coma and was placed on life-support with little chance of recovery. Yvonne phoned my mother for advice. Ever the pragmatist, my mother suggested that if it were a question of living well versus surviving in some sort of reduced state, Art would not want the latter.

Freed from the machines keeping him alive, Art lingered for several hours before passing away Nov. 25, 2009. The immediate cause of death was listed as "acute cerebrovascular accident" complicated by "hypertension," "aspirated pneumonia," and "diabetes."

He was 71.

The new garage. The floor of the old garage is still visible, cracked and uneven.

19

CAMOUFLAGE GARAGE

Mable Gulley-Harvey

Through much of our married life Bob regularly held down two jobs. Once we had settled into our permanent home on 11th street in Moline, he would put in an eight-hour shift at the International Harvester Farmall Works and after dinner would do auto repairs in our garage.

During winters he purchased kerosene at the Wareco service station in Rock Island, enough to fill an outdoor barrel that funneled fuel to a heater inside the garage. After igniting it he would head to the house where I would have supper cooked. By the time he was ready to work the garage would be warm.

He might labor into the night until a job was finished, or stretch the repairs over several days. After he shut down for the evening he would catch the 10 o'clock news on television before bed. By 6:30 the next morning he was on his way to the factory for another eight-hour shift.

It was a routine he followed for two decades.

Bob always talked about adding a second bay to the cramped one-car garage that barely allowed him room between his tool bench and the vehicle he was working on. Because the cement was uneven he struggled to open and close the big bay doors to the alley. The locks on the bottom were pull-chain latches that any enterprising thief with a handy screwdriver could pry open with minimal effort. I worried that someone would run off with expensive tools that took Bob a lifetime to acquire.

I wanted our property to look better and had visions of Bob attaching shack-like outbuildings to an already dilapidated structure. Our lot was 150' X 60,' with plenty of space to accommodate a brand-new building minus the current eyesore of our one-car garage.

My brothers were all excellent carpenters—two had built their own homes—so I approached them about constructing a two-car garage with ample room for Bob's tools and a workbench. I suspected, given his cautious penny-pinching nature, Bob never would agree so I devised a plan for the project to be done without his knowledge.

Velma Harvey-Marr studies a copy of the comic fanzine "Sense of Wonder" while husband Vernon Marr tackles Jim Steranko's "History of Comics, Volume I."

Bob's factory always shut down for two weeks in July and all the employees took vacation at the same time. I figured this offered the perfect window to erect a new garage, provided I could get Bob away from the Quad-Cities so my brothers could build. I quietly purchased a permit from the city and signed three blank checks for my mother, with instructions and a budget for my brothers.

* * * * * * * * *

Bob's Aunt Velma and Uncle Vernon Marr were teachers who resided in Brawley, California, near the Mexican border. We always had an open invitation to visit. So with Brad in tow we headed west, marveling at the numerous slot machines on display in Reno and visiting San Francisco where they happened to be filming an episode of the then-popular television series "The Streets of San Francisco." We nearly lost Brad when the cable car we had boarded began to lurch forward without him and he frantically crawled between the legs of the conductor who shouted his disapproval.

After walking Fisherman's Wharf and mingling with a caricature artist, we looked at Alcatraz across the bay. While Bob waited outside I took Brad and entered a bookstore near the hotel we were staying, not realizing it was restricted to adults only. Just as Brad in his innocence began to kneel down and thumb through a magazine with three nude men on the front cover, the proprietor yelled, "Hey lady, get that kid out of here!"

The next day we journeyed across the Golden Gate Bridge. On trips I was always the navigator but this time I gave Bob bad directions on purpose so we could make a U-turn and cross the bridge twice. I was quietly mailing postcards back to my mother in Illinois, inquiring about my brothers' progress with the new garage. We made a brief stop at Disneyland, later donating the remainder of our tickets to a couple of sailors entering just as we were leaving.

Our Oldsmobile had no air conditioner, so we were traveling with every window down in an attempt to keep cool in the unbearable heat. When we pulled into Velma and Vernon's driveway, a lizard scurrying across the stucco of the house caught my eye. Seeing our red faces, Velma nearly yanked us out of the car and proceeded to rush us into their air-conditioned home.

Velma and Vernon taught English to school children just over the border in Mexico. They took us on a day trip to Mexicali, a Mexican city just across from Calexico, California. We haggled with vendors over souvenirs and hid our disgust at the open barrels of fried chicken rotting in the sun amid clouds of black flies. Brad found two Spanish comics, "Los Fantasticos" (a knock-off of his favorite, "The Fantastic Four") and another detailing the exploits of a turban-clad superhero called Kali-Man. We adjourned to a Chinese restaurant for a meal, finding humor in being Americans eating Asian food in a Mexican city.

Our hosts drove us out to the desert where we watched people in dune buggies race across the terrain like drunken drivers. Brad spent an hour climbing atop the dunes until his eyes got so full of sand he had to flush them out under the shower so he could open them.

Saying our goodbyes to Velma and Vernon the next day we headed to Needles, California, through the Mojave Desert. It was 118 degrees and we spotted only one other vehicle along the desert highway—while Bob was changing a flat a family in a sedan pulled up and asked if we needed help. It was the pre-cellphone era and anyone stranded for very long was courting heat stroke or worse.

* * * * * * * * *

Back in Moline, rainy weather had stalled construction of the new garage the first week of our trip. Once the cement flooring finally had been poured, Don, Bobby and Billy Bob managed to erect the garage during the second week, in between all their other commitments.

I had instructed them to mount the two bay doors along the side facing the old garage instead of having them open onto the alley which left little room be-

Robert Harvey Jr says goodbye to cousin Jerry Cook in front of his new garage, while his old garage (next door) awaits demolition.

tween the two structures. My reasons would become apparent.

On the day of our return Bob drove right past our house. The new garage had thrown off his sense of direction. After he circled the block, he parked, got out and pondered this structure he was seeing for the first time.

"It's your new garage," I offered by way of understatement.

He walked around it, taking note of the narrow span between the two buildings and where my brothers had placed the two bay doors.

"But you can't get a car into it," he said, still wondering how my brothers could have made such a horrific design error. "There's not enough room between the two garages!"

"There will be when you tear the old garage down," I countered, my logic becoming clear.

(With additional material by Brad Harvey.)

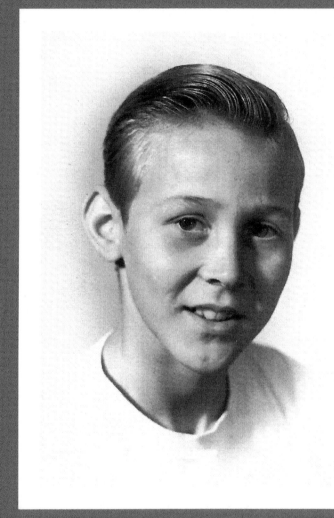

Billy Bob Gulley

20
SELF~MADE

Brad Harvey

I had two uncles named Bill and each characterized the differences between the Harveys and the Gulleys.

Bill Harvey was formally educated, a doctor, a resolute man of faith and a pillar of the hometown he never left. The kind who ended up with a building named in his honor.

By contrast, the Gulleys inspired no plaques or public honors. None of the brothers graduated high school and most entered factories at young ages—it was an era when strong labor unions or having a skill set were enough to cover a working man from cradle to grave.

Bill Gulley—or, less formally, Billy Bob—was clearly an anomaly to his siblings in temperament and ambitions. My uncle Don once declared of Billy Bob, "He's not a Gulley, he's an Aaron!" perceiving his younger brother's independence and self-confidence as arrogance, a trait he associated with their mother's side of the family. In life and in business the Aarons seldom made missteps, something Don and his other brothers must have quietly envied given their own stumbles.

Billy Bob's business acumen and its rewards inspired awe among the rest of us. We marveled at the steady stream of new trucks he drove, the fancy homes he built for himself and his willingness to take spectacular financial risks while we puttered along boring but predictable career paths.

But Don, never one to let an Achilles Heel go unaddressed, pointed out Billy Bob's weakness: a reliance on antacids when the stresses of a business deal converged on his brother's digestive tract. The notoriously tight-fisted Don would go on to purchase an apartment building post-retirement and become a landlord, something no one could have imagined without the influence of his wheeler-dealer younger brother leading by example.

* * * * * * * * *

For the youngest Gulley brother who aspired to the good life, getting there was not easy.

He entered the world Oct. 30, 1941, weighing in at more than 13 pounds. My mother, enthralled by a drummer/classmate named Billy Bob, bestowed the moniker on her new baby brother. In a family of literal giants (the Gulley brothers were all more than six feet tall) the last child of Lawrence and Josie Gulley soon would tower over the rest at six feet six inches.

Billy Bob Gulley, age 10

Aside from being terrorized by the occasional bully and rescued by his protective older brothers (Lawrence Edward and Arthur Lee once dispatched a tormentor by beating and then leaving the tough tied to a tree in the woods) his early years were uneventful. He started working odd jobs at age 13. At 15, he bought himself a horse, the first of many in what became a life-long passion.

After the sudden death of his father when Billy Bob was 17—Billy Bob being the sole Gulley offspring living at home— his widowed mother rented out their Matherville house and the two moved to a Milan apartment before eventually taking up residence in Moline.

Eschewing formal education, Billy Bob hit the streets in search of serious employment. He began a two-year sheet-metal apprenticeship with Modern Heating, an East Moline heating and air-conditioning company. "I didn't set out to work in that type of business, they were just the first place that hired me," he noted. His ambition got the better of him when he was caught moonlighting—in violation of company policy—and was fined for the infraction. The incident further fueled his natural inclination to be sole boss. Leaving Modern Heating after nine years, he founded Bill's Heating and Air Conditioning.

Typical of any cash-poor start-up he struggled, but what he lacked in funding he made up with front. He would often show up on new building sites before ground had been broken to ingratiate himself to contractors, more often than not winning their business away from older, more established companies.

"It was up and down for the first five years," he recalls, gauging his success by "the fewer number of hot dogs I was forced to eat during the lean times." He stuck to his original business model, keeping the number of employees down to a minimum, thereby ensuring he took only the jobs he wanted versus taking on work he disliked to meet the demands of a bigger payroll.

At age 21 he secured a $500 loan and, despite his lack of experience, built the first of seven homes. "If you're a poor kid without money but want something, your only chance at owning anything is to make it yourself," he states, adding that he can't remember the address of that first home other than that it was located in Milan. As his business grew the houses became bigger, with swimming pools and an indoor riding rink as he further indulged his passion for quarter horses.

Billy Bob met Judie Bussman, his first wife, at Deb's Drive-In, the Milan root beer stand where she worked while attending high school (not surprisingly, their memories differ over where that first meeting occurred— Judie recalls it was at a nearby riding stable where she first encountered "bad boy" Bill Gulley). He and his friends offered her a ride after work but left her stranded on the other side of town, forcing her to walk home alone in the middle of the night.

After her father's job with Goodyear necessitated a transfer to Des Moines, Iowa, Judie briefly attended school in Iowa City while continuing her long-distance relationship with Billy Bob. Disappointed with the writing curriculum, Judie left after a semester (she would eventually become a published writer and author with three books to her credit). On one of their first dates they took in the film "Psycho" which so unnerved Billy Bob that on the way back from dropping Judie off at her dorm, the drowsy

Billy Bob Gulley takes a break.

suitor decided to park his car at a bustling truck stop rather than sleep alone in the park. They married in 1960, raising two sons (Ronnie and Jeff, in order of birth) who followed Billy Bob into the family business. With their mutual love of horses, Billy Bob and Judie would fill their bookcases with numerous trophies won at weekend horse shows, a lifestyle they would follow for years.

* * * * * * * * *

When Billy Bob was 56 he suffered his first major heart attack. Under doctor's orders, he retired from the business, putting his oldest son Ronnie in charge and taking a cash draw from the coffers. "It was the years and years of mental stress pil-

ing up and knowing that there were at least three families counting on my company to keep everyone's bills paid," he says today.

Further health issues and divorce would soon decimate what always had remained a family-owned company. Billy Bob betrays a slight bitterness that what took a lifetime to build was eventually sold at a loss.

These days, if you want to engage his attention, switch the topic to—what else?—horses. With his longtime com-

Billy Bob Gulley

panion Connie (whom he married in 2017) he's busy following his latest investment around the horse-show circuits and avenues like the American RFD-TV Rodeo. His horse's rankings have been impressive enough for Billy Bob to turn down offers on the animal worth thousands of dollars. He keeps a schedule that might bend the knees of a lesser man his age, let alone one that still suffers from chronic health problems.

"You have to keep going," he states without a trace of irony, blowing off the notion that you have any other options at this late stage.

Ruby and Joe Aaron seated on their front porch with Mable Gulley-Harvey.

CODA

Brad Harvey

Aunt Ruby lost her beloved husband Joe Dec. 1, 1984, after he'd been hospitalized for what should have been a minor procedure related to his kidneys. As a widow, Ruby continued to reside at the longtime family home on St. George and West Church in West City for many years until her own failing health made it unsafe for her to remain alone.

Selfless as ever and not wishing to burden others with her care, Ruby voluntarily checked herself into the Severin Intermediate Care Home in Benton. She refused to look back, walking away from her house, its possessions and a lifetime of memories. She would pass away on Aug. 10, 2007 at age 95, having outlived her husband, brother and one of her three sons. Developers bought the modest house she had shared with Joe and her family for more than 50 years and leveled it for a new Burger King restaurant.

On Jan. 25, 2018, West City police were called to a home in the 400 block of South Central Street where they found the bodies of Joe and Ruby's eldest son Billy Gene and his wife Wilma Louise. Both had died from

Billy Gene and Wilma Louise Aaron in younger years.

gunshot wounds in an apparent murder-suicide. Billy Gene was 86 and the couple had been experiencing severe health issues.

* * * * * * * * *

My uncle Don once recalled what a night going to the movies entailed for an impoverished family of nine, laughing uproariously at how he and his siblings would pile into a horse-drawn wagon—outfitted with rubber tires by their father—and make the trek from the deep countryside to the nearest movie theater in Benton.

"You talk about a load of goony, grinning hillbillies," he noted, still amused by the memory decades later.

For my mother, crawling out of her father's homemade contraption amid the parked cars and the judgmental gaze of the other movie-goers, it was one more public humiliation to be endured. She felt her family's indigence each time she donned the uniform of welfare-issued sack dresses and shoes or adjourned to her school's basement so her classmates wouldn't see the egg sandwich she'd brought from home in lieu of a school-provided lunch her father could not afford.

In addition, although she loved her family, as the oldest and only girl she was often an unwilling substitute parent to a rambunctious brood of boys when her own mother became otherwise distracted and overwhelmed.

Perhaps because she had spent so many years on the economic and societal periphery it imbued my mother—and my father by association—with a keen sense of empathy toward others less fortunate. They bought groceries for down-on-their-luck relatives and took nieces and nephews on vacation. They covered rent and mortgages. For one impoverished aunt, a hairstylist by trade, they purchased an expensive barber chair so she could operate out of her home without leaving her kids. A cousin was able to reunite cross-country with his estranged father thanks to my parents purchasing an airline ticket.

On infrequent Sundays my mother would, albeit reluctantly, entertain the wife of one of my father's friends. Boorish and self-absorbed, the woman would linger for hours re-telling the same gossipy tales. "She doesn't seem to have anyone else to talk to," my mother would offer in the woman's defense. After her death my parents loaned her husband $5,000 for funeral expenses. The husband died a few years later, the debt unpaid.

Upon her retirement from the Moline Public Library my mother found herself at loose ends. She volunteered to work with the elderly at a nearby adult daycare facility that eventually morphed into a full-time paying position. When that endeavor ended, she joined my uncle Bobby, his wife Donna and my cousin Ronnie Gulley on a two-week trip to the south to build houses for Habitat for Humanity.

A series of small strokes and related health issues slowed my mother near the completion of this book. Although not as robust physically as she once was, her mind and speech remain unaffected by recent events. Her tongue is as sharp as ever, particularly when reminding overzealous physical therapists pulling and prodding her limbs that she's almost 90.

* * * * * * * * *

In July of 2018 my father celebrated his 92nd birthday. He's still driving and climbing ladders. When he and my mother attended their respective high school reunions in Thompsonville several years ago, my father was one of the sole surviving members of his class and one of the few unencumbered with a cane, walker or wheelchair.

When I remarked to him, with a measure of humor and sarcasm, "Wow, you must have been voted most likely to outlive your classmates," he laughed, much as he always has at my jokes, good or bad.

ACKNOWLEDGMENTS

When we began compiling these stories in 2010—the gestation period extended well into 2018—we were adamant our words pass through the hands of an experienced editor. Linda Cook has been a godsend, wielding her red pen with a measure of impunity and boundless enthusiasm for our little project. That she did it for such a pittance is even more remarkable!

Joyce Harvey was involved in the pre-production of this book, scanning several hundred photographs and digitally restoring many of the images originally deemed unsalvageable. Her proofreading, organization and correction skills are formidable plus she understands computer voodoo in a way that the authors do not.

We knew we had chosen a winner in graphic design artist John Sellards when we saw the first mock-ups for the cover of this book. Check him out online at John Sellards Design.

A lengthy scroll through Amazon.com better explains the voluminous output of writer extraordinaire Max Allan Collins. He remains a local legend in our neck of the woods, a guiding light for many first-time authors who have benefitted from his hard-won wisdom and advice. His rock band Crusin' was just inducted into Iowa's Rock and Roll Hall of Fame.

Christopher Allen Gulley and Sue Gulley-Winters dug deep into their memory banks and their photo collections to provide us with unseen images of their respective parents. Ray Congrove took the wonderful photograph of Robert and Mable Harvey on the eve of their 70th wedding anniversary.

Ken Sharp offered his expertise regarding self-publishing. He writes amazing books on music and produces joyous pop music for a worldwide legion of fans.

And finally, the authors wish to recognize Jill Harvey-Flowers. With her unflagging energy and selfless concern for others, she has inherited the title of family caregiver—Aunt Ruby would be proud.

ABOUT THE AUTHORS

MABLE GULLEY-HARVEY has kept journals and written short stories much of her life. A voracious reader, she lives in a house full of books. She started piano lessons in her eighties and knows more about Keith Richards and Pete Townshend than most her age. She gardens, enjoys British murder mysteries on PBS and considers "Judge Judy" a guilty pleasure.

BRAD HARVEY is a musician, writer and trucker on any given day. A fervent Anglophile he collects music biographies, favors a good Joe Strummer lyric and rates The Jam as his number-one band.